Sight translation, sight interpreting meeting at the cross modes: Sign language interpreters as translators

Proceedings of the efsli Conference
Vietri sul Mare, Italy, 16th-18th September 2011

Edited by Anna Cardinaletti

European Forum of Sign Language Interpreters
2012

ISBN 9789081306539

© European Forum of Sign Language Interpreters, 2012

Edited by: Anna Cardinaletti
Cover design by: Triin Jõeveer
Printed by: *Createspace*

This publication is made possible with the support of the EU Lifelong Learning Programme.

All rights reserved
No part of this publication may be produced, stored in a retrieval system or transmitted in any form or any means (electronic, photocopying, recording or otherwise), without the prior written permission of the publisher.

Foreword

For the first time in the history of the European Forum of Sign Language Interpreters (efsli), the annual conference was held in Italy from 16th – 18th September 2011. The conference was hosted and organised by the Italian Association of Sign Language Interpreters (ANIOS) in beautiful Vietri sul Mare on the Amalfi coast.

These proceedings provide you an in depth overview of the presentations held at the conference on the topic of 'Sight translation and sight interpretation, meeting at the cross modes'. The conference presentations were selected by the scientific committee, chaired by Marco Nardi, member of ANIOS and former efsli President. I also hereby would like to thank Anna Cardinaletti, the editor of these proceedings, who together with the editorial committee reviewed the articles.

The organising committee welcomed over 250 participants from 25 countries. The participants were treated to a wonderful and inspiring conference in Italian style. The efsli AGM and conference would not have been possible without all the volunteers who contributed to our event. We really appreciate their efforts and dedication.

On behalf of the efsli board, I would also like to thank all the participants: together with the presenters and the volunteers you helped make efsli2011 so successful.

Maya de Wit

efsli President

Table of contents

Contributors   7

Introduction   11
Anna Cardinaletti

The use of the focus question in sight translation. The case of LIS   15
Carmela Bertone

Phased by translation: identifying the challenges and solutions in sight interpretation   23
Sarah Bown and Kristiaan Dekesel

Translating poetry   35
Valeria Buonomo and Pietro Celo

Sight translation with meaning in a signing world   51
Sharon Neumann Solow

Deaf translator: a new profession. Context and limits   59
Julia Pelhate

Requirements for translating films, in a multimedia context, from German into German sign language   69
Knut Weinmeister

Abstracts   81

How should a sign language interpreter prepare to perform a sight interpretation of a signed text?   83
Giuseppe Amorini

Sight translation and sign language translation: two young and eager cousins of sign language interpreting?   84
Stuart Anderson and Donna Ruane-Cauchi

**Interpreting scripted speeches: An examination of expert interpreters
85**
Daniel Gile, Brenda Nicodemus, Laurie Swabey and Marty Taylor

Sign language translation as cooperative action: A theoretical model and an example from practice   86
Nadja Grbic, Karin Hofstätter and Christian Stalzer

About the contributors   88

Contributors

Giuseppe Amorini
amorus18@hotmail.it
Italy

Stuart Anderson
stuart@signamic.co.uk
Signamic Ltd
UK

Carmela Bertone
bertone@unive.it
Dipartimento di Studi linguistici e culturali comparati
Università Ca' Foscari Venezia
Italy

Sarah Bown
s.bown@wlv.ac.uk
Department of World and Sign Languages
School of Law, Social Sciences and Communication
University of Wolverhampton
UK

Valeria Buonomo
valeria.buonomo@gmail.com
Italy

Anna Cardinaletti
cardin@unive.it
Dipartimento di Studi linguistici e culturali comparati
Università Ca' Foscari Venezia
Italy

Pietro Celo
pietro.celo@libero.it, pietro.celo@unimib.it
Italy

Kristiaan Dekesel
k.dekesel@wlv.ac.uk
Department of World and Sign Languages
School of Law, Social Sciences and Communication
University of Wolverhampton
UK

Daniel Gile
daniel.gile@yahoo.com
Université Université Sorbonne Nouvelle - Paris 3
École Supérieure d'Interprètes et de Traducteurs (ESIT)
Centre Universitaire Dauphine
France

Nadja Grbic
nadja.grbic@uni-graz.at
University of Graz
Institut für Translationswissenschaft
Austria

Karin Hofstätter
karin.hofstaetter@uni-graz.at
University of Graz
Institut für Translationswissenschaft
Austria

Sharon Neumann Solow
SNSBear@gmail.com
USA

Brenda Nicodemus
brenda.nicodemus@gallaudet.edu
Department of Interpretation
Gallaudet University
USA

Julia Pelhate
julia.pelhate@websourd.org
WebSourd
France

Donna Ruane-Cauchi
donnamrsli@aol.com
Signamic Ltd
UK

Christian Stalzer
christian.stalzer@uni-graz.at
University of Graz
Institut für Translationswissenschaft
Austria

Laurie Swabey
laswabey@stkate.edu
Interpreting Department
St. Catherine University
USA

Marty Taylor
mtaylor@connect.ab.ca
Interpreting Consolidated
Canada

Knut Weinmeister
Knut.Weinmeister@gebaerdenwerk.de
Germany

Introduction

Anna Cardinaletti

This volume contains the contributions delivered at the efsli Annual Conference held in Vietri sul Mare on 16th-18th September 2011. Unfortunately, not all contributors were able to prepare papers for the volume. In that case, we have collected the abstract submitted for the conference or a revised version of it.

The volume represents the interesting and novel discussions from many of the questions raised by sight translation on the one hand and by the emerging figure of the Deaf translator on the other.

More than one contributor underline the need of further discussion on sight translation when one of the two languages involved is a sign language. Specific questions are raised by the visual modality of sign languages and by the fact that these languages do not have a written form. At the same time, many authors observe that the best potential translators, particularly in the case of sight translation, are Deaf translators because of their native knowledge of their respective sign languages. Being a native signer does not however suffice, as in the case of translation into any language. The need for a specific training, in sign language translation, is pointed out by almost every contributor. The experiences they report also show that the situation in the status of training and working conditions of Deaf and hearing sign language translators is different in the various countries represented in the volume. The positive experiences collated in these proceedings can therefore also count as a model for those countries that are yet to develop service provision in sign language translation, in order to achieve full access to information and education for the Deaf communities in any country.

The following is a brief summary of the contributions to the conference.

Giuseppe Amorini presents his experience as Deaf translator in two different situations: written texts such as books and subtitled television programmes, in front of an audience of Deaf people with low literacy skills. The latter is an interesting case of sight translation, in which images can help the translators in their work. Translation becomes a support to what is being watched.

Stuart Anderson and Donna Ruane-Cauchi discuss the issues raised by the wider demands of sight translation and pointed out that a full qualification for sign language translation is timely and needed. They present on the contents of their interpreting courses in UK and how this new profession may open up new job opportunities in the future.

Carmela Bertone discusses the focalisation strategy used in sign languages, namely that of using a question in order to introduce a focus into the discourse. She points out that this construction should not be considered informal as it would be in the case of spoken languages, in which it is often adopted as a narrative strategy used by or for children. Not possessing a written form, sign languages do not display the register stratification found in languages with a written tradition. Bertone instead suggests that the question-focus strategy is particularly appropriate in the case of sight translations since it allows breaking down long sentences, typical of written texts, into shorter and simpler phrases.

Sarah Bown and Kristiaan Dekesel present a pilot study aimed to establish how widespread the use of sight translation is within the day-to-day practice of sign language interpreters. Through a questionnaire distributed to translation and interpreting agencies in UK, they could conclude that it is indeed service in much demand. They also suggest that a module of sight translation should be included in sign language interpreter training programmes and enriched by Think Aloud Protocols to document the thought processes of interpreters during the sight translation process.

Valeria Buonomo and Pietro Celo's contribution focuses on the general issue of translating poetry and on the more specific issue of translating poetry into sign language, which implies intersemiotic translation. They discuss in detail the choices made while translating Primo Levi's poem *Se questo è un uomo* into Italian Sign Language.

While raising the issue of the increasing demand of translating formal, public speeches, which are fully constructed prior to delivery and therefore display linguistic properties different from spontaneous communication, **Daniel Gile, Brenda Nicodemus, Laurie Swabey and**

Marty Taylor present an experiment with experienced interpreters, who after interpreting Barack Obama's inaugural speech into ASL, viewed their videotaped interpretation and engaged in a retrospective Think Aloud Protocol (TAP) about their work. Gile, Nicodemus, Swabey and Taylor also discussed the implications for interpreter training programmes, on both the theoretical and the practical level.

Nadja Grbic, Karin Hofstätter and Christian Stalzer instead centre their attention on collaborative translation, which was used for the translation of a website into Austrian Sign Language. The team was composed of both hearing and Deaf translators.

Sharon Neumann Solow's paper is a very detailed introduction to sight translation and the specific properties this process displays when one of the two languages is a sign language. She also discusses several strategies and techniques that can help the translator/interpreter being more effective.

A Deaf translator herself, Julia Pelhate discusses the many questions raised by this emergent profession in France especially in view of the fact that no or too little specific support is provided by education and training. The only 5 qualified Deaf translators in France are all employed by the company WebSourd, who thus have to answer those many questions while producing the translations themselves. She also points out that translations are a means to fight low literacy skills, still found in too high percentages among Deaf people in France as well as in other European countries. A text in sign language proposed together with the original text in written French may allow Deaf people to deepen their knowledge of French and to increase access to culture and information.

The final paper by Knut Weinmeister discusses the many competences that translators in general and sign language translators in particular, must have in order to provide high quality translations and focuses on the additional competences required for translating in a multimedia context.

The conference was also enriched by the talk entitled *From text into sign in different discourse modes: information reception, processing and production* by the invited speaker, Christian Rathmann, and by the following poster presentations:

Jens Heßmann (Germany), Eeva Salmi (Finland), Graham H. Turner (Scotland – UK) and Svenja Wurm (Germany/Scotland/Finland), *From EUMASLI to EUMASLIT? Placing sight interpretation and translation in the context of a European master programme in sign language interpreting*;

Paul Michaels (England – UK), *The answer is in the question: the difficulties in interpreting multiple-choice question examination situations*;

Anna-Lena Nilsson (Sweden) and Maya Rohdell (Sweden), *What should I write?: Some do's and don'ts when translating signed corpus material for the web*;

Raija Roslof (Finland), *Translation, spoken and signed language collaborating in sign language interpreter studies*;

Cynthia Roy (USA), *Teaching the history of sign language interpreting and sight translation*;

Anna M.J. Wiener (Austria), *The difference between translation and interpreting in sign language. Specific problems of written text transfer in Austrian Sign Language – A case study*.

All presenters and contributors to this volume have made the 2011 edition of the efsli conference a very useful and enriching opportunity to deepen the knowledge about the specific properties of translation into sign language and the skills required to professionals working in this relatively new domain. The need for specific training, repeatedly pointed out in the papers, will hopefully inspire those who are in charge of the translation and interpreting programmes in sign languages across Europe and beyond.

In conclusion, I would like to thank the members of the editorial committee, Aleksandra Kalata-Zawlocka, Marco Nardi and Marinella Salami for their help in reviewing the articles, Paul Pryce-Jones for his help with English, and Liivi Hollman for her assistance throughout the editorial process.

The use of the focus question in sight translation. The case of LIS

Carmela Bertone

1. Introduction

Informational focus relates to the distinction between what is given and what is new in a discourse. Natural languages can realize informational focus in different ways: Sometimes it is not grammatically realized, other times it is.

Italian Sign Language (LIS), like several other sign languages and like oral languages, often realizes focus via an interrogative sentence that spotlights the new information. In the sentence *John is washing his car*, *John* is the given information while *washing his car* or *his car* is the new information.

The focus can be introduced by a question: *What is John washing?* This structure is commonly called "rhetorical question" even if it is "neither rhetorical nor question". Observing its prosodic and syntactic properties in ASL, Wilbur (1995) has argued that it has a focusing function like the pseudocleft or wh-cleft structures in other languages.

The aim of this paper is to re-examine the use of this structure that appears to be functional to translation, especially when it must be quick and effective, as is the case in sight translation.

2. Interpretation, translation, and sight translation

Interpretation and translation are not synonymous. In interpretation, a message is taken from a *source* language and, following a selection of the most appropriate vocabulary and syntactic structures, it is rendered in an equivalent message in a different, *target* language. In translation, the transfer of meaning is rendered from a written or recorded text into another similar text, but in this case the translator takes time to produce an accurate message with a real equivalence of meaning with respect to emotion, tone, culture, and language. Translating into LIS involves the transposition of a written text into a sign language (SL) by filming the sign language. The recording enables the translator to control the production in SL. The errors can be detected, corrected, and re-filmed, as happens in a translation into a written text.

Sight translation combines interpretation and translation because the interpreter must very often render a written source-language document into a signed target-language document. In other words, a written text must be translated into an "oral text", with "oral text" meaning "signed text."

Sign language is a non-alphabetic language because it lacks a shared written form, although efforts in creating one are in progress. In this sense, the linguistic constructions of LIS are more similar to an oral text than a written text. The next section will provide some clarifications on this topic.

3. Alphabetic and non-alphabetic languages between written texts and oral texts

Halliday (1989) considers writing a specific system developed in a specific way for alphabetic languages. Alphabetic languages are human languages in which the symbols reflect the pronunciation of the words. Written texts are the result of the mental elaboration of a speaking community that led to specific properties in orthography, linguistic structures, and communication. For this reason, alphabetic languages have specific properties that must be taken into account in the transposition of language codes. In translation, non-alphabetic languages are not considered because the majority of oral languages used in translation are alphabetic. Sign languages are a sort of hybrid category because they are used and disseminated in signing communities that exist within a larger community of speakers, most of whom use the written form.

In this sense, translation into sign language requires specific studies in order to examine two different aspects: the first concerns the transposition of written texts into recorded video-texts from a technical point of view; the second, and more complex aspect, concerns the analysis of specific structures of the written language that must be translated into a language whose structures are closer to spoken languages.

Some aspects of the problems connected with the techniques regarding the transposition of written texts into recorded video-texts (e.g. prompts, memorizing), the transposition of the lexicon (e.g. choice of regional words for places, art terms, etc.), and the choice of the most appropriate syntactic constructions have been treated in Danese, Bertone, Faria (2010a, 2010b).

In this study, more attention will be paid to the analysis of certain structures of the written language that require specific attention in translation. To understand which structures of the written language may present difficulties, it is useful to take a closer look at the differences between written and spoken languages.

Halliday (1989) views written languages as a product and oral languages as a process. This interpretation can be applied to different aspects. First of all, written texts do not require an interlocutor; they are fixed in a form and do not change over time. In this sense, a written text is fixed and static, every word is the result of reasoning, and that is why it is meaningful. Reading makes it possible to go back and re-read. Writing is secondary to thought. In other words, to be effective in writing requires a knowledge of the tools and a structuring of thought. As a consequence, language in the written form can be analysed in ways that only recently have become possible for oral languages.

On the other hand, in oral languages the activity of thought is expressed in real time. For this reason, the language is more fluid, and the meanings of the words are more flexible. Spoken language is used in conversation, there are more interlocutors, and because of this it is more difficult to control and study. While subordination is predominant in written language, in oral language coordination is prevalent, subordination being limited to fewer clauses. Halliday observes: "spoken language is characterized by complex sentence structures with low lexical density (more clauses, but fewer high content words per clause), written language by simple sentence structures with high lexical density (more high content words per clause but fewer clauses)" (Halliday 1979: 114).

4. Sign languages and spoken languages

SLs share more characteristics with spoken languages than with written languages. For example, SLs generally use coordinate structures and not subordinate ones, use repetitions and reduplications (e.g. for the production of plurals, to express iterative or repetitive activities or events, etc.), are used among many interlocutors. It is only recently that SLs can be video-recorded. At first sight, it appears that the language of video-recorded production is more thorough and precise, but it is not structurally different from signed language used in conversation.

Take for instance the system of verbal inflection for person which involves "role taking". The category of person is related to participation in the speech event or the roles of speaker and person being spoken to. While first and second person refer to the speaker and the interlocutor, respectively, third person refers to a person who is not taking part in the discourse. Third person is differentiated in many languages by different qualities (gender, animacy, etc.). In SLs, the speaker can embody the animated third person. That is to say, the first person can be third person: the change of person is indicated by a shift in the speaker's gaze which moves from the interlocutor to another point of space. This is widespread in spoken languages, too. Spoken languages also signal a change of person through voice intonation. That is why sign languages are more emphatic and participatory and not objective and "cold" like written languages.

Another structure that assimilates sign languages to spoken languages is the use of interrogative sentences to introduce new information into the discourse. It means the focus is introduced by an interrogative sentence. This property is discussed in the next section.

5. Focus in sign languages

In a discourse, the part of a sentence that expresses the core of attention or assertion of the utterance is identified as Focus. It is the part of discourse that is not presupposed, it is the comment on a topic, it is what it is said about a certain subject. Focus is the new information. Considering the sentence: *John is washing his car*, *John* is the information known, what he is washing (*his car*) is the new information.

Focus can be highlighted by intonation or syntactically (or both, as in English *HIS CAR, John is washing, not Mary's car,* capital letters signalling the change of intonation). Clefting introduces an obligatory intonation break. In storytelling, it is very common to introduce new information with an interrogative sentence: *What did the wolf do next? What is John washing?*

In LIS, the most apparent system for introducing new information is the interrogative sentence (see Wilbur 1995 for ASL), as in the following examples:

(1) IX_{1p} DEAF, BORN WHERE? ROME

        I am deaf, I was born in Rome.

(2) IX_{2p} WALK UNTIL IX_{2p} SEE WHAT? BAR

        You walk until you see a bar.

This kind of interrogative sentence is aimed at shifting the attention of the interlocutor to the new information. The interruption of discourse and the introduction of questions create new forms of coordinates within the speech to better interpret the subsequent utterance. Observing the prosodic and syntactic properties of these constructions in ASL, Wilbur (1995) has argued that interrogative focusing functions like pseudocleft or wh-cleft structures in other languages. For example, the sentence *I wanted to study art* is a simple sentence. The focalization of new information can be rendered in a complex sentence with a main clause and a dependent one: *What I wanted to study was art.* This kind of construction is recognized as being closer to the spoken rather than the written form.

Ajello (1997) observes that the phenomenon of using the interrogative form to introduce the focus is typical of storytelling in oral languages (e.g. Italian dialects). In this sense, oral languages and sign languages can be viewed as less formal and "more colloquial" than written texts.

In sign languages, the use of the interrogative form to introduce a new topic into the discourse is commonly considered very informal, probably because it is typical of a child's narrative register in spoken languages. Generally, the closer a text is to the written form, the more formal it is considered. This classification cannot be applied to sign languages because they have no written form. They use the interrogative form in a specific way, which is focalization.

6. The use of the interrogative form in sight translation

A complex concept from one language should be rendered in the target language by choosing the most appropriate vocabulary to faithfully render the source message in a linguistically, emotionally, tonally, and culturally equivalent target message.

In sight translation, interpreters often do not have time to reorganize the sentence into more effective constructions. Consider for instance the following passage:

(3)   *Early the next morning, in company with the Town Councillors, the Mayor was walking in the square below.* ["The Happy Prince" by Oscar Wilde]

In translation, it is necessary to put the subject of the sentence at the beginning of the sentence. If someone is reading the text, it can be difficult to wait and to have to keep all the information in mind. Using a sign language structure, we can focalize the information by breaking the sentence down into phrases via the use of a question, as in (4):

(4)   *Early the next morning, in company with the Town Councillors, Who was walking in the square below? The Mayor*

Let's look at another example, an argumentative text:

(5)   *The Committee decided to inscribe this property on the basis of criteria (III), (IV) and (V), considering that the impressive remains of the towns of Pompei and Herculaneum and their associated villas, buried by the eruption of Vesuvius in AD 79, provide a complete and vivid picture of society and daily life at a specific moment in the past that is without parallel anywhere in the world.* [Justification for inscription of Archaeological Areas of Pompei, Herculaneum and Torre Annunziata]

Interconnected clauses, rich in adjectives and information, make up a complex sentence where the key clause is interrupted by other clauses that provide important explanations for the main clause. In a sight translation of a text of this kind, when it is read, it is impossible to interpret it without breaking it down into shorter and simpler parts. It is important to recognize the function of each clause to make a focalizing question that shifts the focus to all new information:

(6)   *The Committee decided to inscribe this property on the basis of criteria (III), (IV) and (V). What have they considered? The impressive remains of the towns of Pompei and Herculaneum and their associated villas, buried by the eruption of Vesuvius in AD 79, provide a complete and vivid picture of society and daily life. When did it happen? In a specific moment in the past. Why is it so important? Because it is unparallel anywhere in the world.*

6. Conclusion

Sight translation requires a different approach with respect to translation because in sight translation, there is no time to reflect on the text, since it needs to be both rapid and effective. The translation is often from a written text that is read aloud. Written texts are considerably different from oral texts. Since sign languages are more similar to spoken languages, the use of "So-called Rhetorical Questions" to focalize the new information in the discourse is not to be considered informal. Rather, it may be a strategy aimed at rendering a message in the target language in a linguistically, emotionally, tonally, and culturally equivalent form.

References

Ajello R. 1997. Lingue vocali, lingue dei segni e «l'illusion mimétique». In R. Ambrosini, P. Bologna, F. Motta, C. Orlandi (eds.), *Scríbthair a ainm n-ogaim*, Pacini Editore, 17-30.

Danese L., C. Bertone, C. Farìa 2010a. La traduzione dall'italiano alla Lingua dei Segni Italiana (LIS): nuove prospettive di ricerca. In G. Massariello Mcrgagora and S. dal Maso (eds.), *I Luoghi della*

Traduzione le Interfacce. Atti del XLIII Congresso Internazionale di Studi della Società di Linguistica Italiana (SLI), Bulzoni, 223-229.

Danese L., C. Bertone, C. Farìa 2010b. Da dove vieni campagnolo? La traduzione di una guida turistica di Venezia dall'italiano alla lingua dei segni italiana (LIS). Nuove prospettive di ricerca. Paper presented at the international conference "*Emerging Topics in Translation and Interpreting/ Nuovi percorsi in traduzione e interpretazione*", Trieste, June 16-18. In press.

Halliday M.A.K. 1979. Differences between spoken and written language: some implications for litteracy teaching. In G. Page, J. Elkins, B. O'Connor (eds.), *Communication Through Reading: Proceedings of the Fourth Australian Reading Conference*, Adelaide, S.A.: Australian Reading Assosiation, 37-52.

Halliday M.A.K. 1989. *Spoken and written language*. Oxford University Press.

Wilbur R. 1995. Why so-called 'Rethorical Questions' are neither rethorical nor questions? In H.F. Bos and G.M. Shermar (eds.), *Sign Language Research 1994: Proceedings of the fourth European congress on sign language research, Munich 1-3 Sept.*, Hamburg, Signum Press, 149-169.

Phased by translation: identifying the challenges and solutions in sight interpretation

Sarah Bown and Kristiaan Dekesel

1. Introduction

Various academics have argued for the inclusion of sight translation within an interpreter-training programme. However, little formal documented evidence can be found on its actual use within the sign language interpreting community.

This pilot study aims to ascertain how widespread the use of sight translation is within the day to day practice of sign language interpreters, argues for its inclusion in sign language interpreter training programmes, and explores whether we can influence the cognitive processes during the sight translation task undertaken by interpreters in utilising Think Aloud Protocols (TAPs) during the sight translation process. Of particular interest was the distribution of cognitive processes within various areas such as linguistic features, audience consideration, justifications and implications, quality and legal issues, and whether interpreters at varying stages of their training or experience demonstrated different thought patterns whilst undertaking sight translation.

In order to obtain a more accurate perspective on the current use, demand for and provision of sight translation, we contacted several interpreting agencies across the region whilst simultaneously consulting their service provision information as to whether they were offering sight translation. We also interviewed practitioners and community representatives as to the historical developments of the application of sight translation.

2. Sight translations in the day-to-day practice of interpreters

Historically, one of the reasons for the lack of evidence of the use of sight translation within the bookings of interpreting agencies and the day-to-day practice of interpreters, is due to the fact that traditionally deaf people relied on family, friends and non-interpreting professionals, for example welfare workers, social workers, missioners for deaf people, or Deaf people themselves to undertake sight translation:

"March, when the tax forms came was hell... a hundred tax forms to complete or more... hours of work..." (DWEB 2011)

Another reason for its lack of formal evidence is that sight translation assignments appear to 'piggy-back' on other interpreting bookings, meaning that an interpreter booked for particular assignment and having completed it, can and very often is presented with, for example, a letter, form or document and asked to explain or translate it.

The actual service provided by agencies is diverse. It spans from some which offer no formal sight translation service to others which offer multiple sessions per month taking place in an equally diverse range of settings from a dedicated unit, to a drop in service at a local deaf centre, to home visits:

"We run six sessions per month throughout Worcestershire, and two per month in Oxfordshire." (Deaf Direct communication services 2011)

There seems to be a contradiction with regards to the demand for sight translation. Some agencies claim that the demand is low and has historically been so, whilst others state they are inundated with requests for sight translation to the extent that the service is limited by timed appointments and will only cover 'salient' points or extracts. In order for the Deaf client to do so, however, would require a level of understanding of written English pertaining to the document, which may not be the case, as educational attainment studies have shown:

"There is a clear demand for the service... at some sessions the demand is such that deaf people have to be limited to 20 minutes each..." (Deaf Direct Communication Services 2011)

The survey conducted highlighted the types of documents that a service could expect to be brought to them, for example, Disability Living Allowance forms, carer's allowance applications, local authority tenancy agreements, utility bills, arrear letters from banks, credit/debt recovery companies correspondence, medical reports, Special Educational Needs statements, Individual Education Programmes, benefits claims, census data, junk mail, letters from estate agents, council, internet broadband providers, insurance policies and appliance manuals:

"They brought everything that dropped through the letter box" (DWEB 2011)

"... utility bills, medical reports, census forms,..." (coHearentVision 2011)

The professionals carrying out the task of sight translation also raised two areas of concern. Although sight translation is seen as a way of empowering Deaf people, some professionals challenged this view and felt that sight translation prolonged dependency rather than promoting independence. It should also be noted that higher educational literacy attainment would significantly reduce the requirement for sight translation. Secondly, certain demands of the task, for example, subject knowledge and comprehension of context specific concepts, raised issues over legal implications and some practitioners saw this as a challenge to the role the interpreter was able to adopt.

In some instances, preference was given to the social work team to carry out the translation. Where an interpreter was delivering the sight translation and uncertainty regarding the above issues occurred, it was common to reference back to the originator of the document, which in turn altered the sight translation task into a telephone interpreting assignment:

"... the potential consequences of translating documents without the requisite knowledge to enable a safe translation." (coHearentVision 2011)

"...essentially our role is to encourage independence and empower deaf people to have full access to choice." (Deaf Direct Communication Services 2011)

"hours of work and taking away any responsibility for self-responsibility" (DWEB 2011)

3. Sight translation in interpreter training programmes

The usefulness of sight translation as a training tool has not been disputed (Curvers et al. 1986; Weber 1990; Martin 1993; Falbo 1995;

Viaggio 1995; Kim 2001; Agrifoglio 2004; Lambert 2004; Sofer 2006; Sampaio 2007), as it expands an interpreter's specific and general knowledge, supports the development of vocabulary due to its possible application of a wide variety of texts, is a useful pedagogic exercise for expanding an interpreters skill, heightens awareness of strengths and weaknesses, enhances the cognitive processing within translation, can be applied within training programmes in both the early stages and as regular sessions, is in fact often seen as a stepping stone to simultaneous and consecutive interpreting, can be undertaken as an individual or peer/group activity encompassing translation critique, allows for an optimum translation and raises awareness of a diverse range of linguistic features. This, to the extent that some argue that it should be regarded as a separate subject or entity within interpreter training, as it builds a practitioner's repertoire of solutions and strategies for working with complex texts. In contrast, however, we only have sparse guidance on its teaching methodology:

"ST is included in the course I teach because it is an activity that future graduates will probably be required to perform in their professional life..." (Martin 1993:400)

The differences between simultaneous interpreting, consecutive interpreting, sight translation and written translation have been extensively explored (Viezzi 1989a, 1989b,1990; Agrifoglio 2004; Lambert 2004; Pöchhacker 2004; Biela-Wolońciej 2007; Jiménez Ivars 2008; Dragsted and Hansen 2009).

Agrifoglio (2004) provides a succinct overview of these distinct differences and many have concluded that sight translation can best be seen as a hybrid form. Sight translation provides a range of advantages compared to other modes of interpreting, such as unrestricted access to the source language, translator controlled pace, but also involves risks in particular in relation to source text interference on the target language due to its constant presence.

In accordance with Gile's Effort Models (Gile 1985, 1995, 2002), translation demands 'mental energy' of which he argues we have a finite amount. As trainers, we were keen to explore the extent to which we could influence and control the cognitive processes within this mental energy when practitioners were undertaking sight translation. What we also wished to ascertain, was where this finite energy was being assigned, i.e. which areas within the thinking process, and more importantly, could we increase the amount of finite energy or, influence the areas it was being applied to (prioritisation). We embarked on utilising Think Aloud Protocols to document the thought processes of interpreters during the sight translation process and were specifically interested at looking for a way in which to influence the development of interpreting skills amongst beginners.

In contrast to studies that focus on translation errors or failures within the final product of sight translation, we wanted to focus on the thoughts within the translation process that would inform us of the thinking behind the decisions that led to a successful or unsuccessful outcome. In other words, the thought processes that avoided or caused translation failures.

4. The research

Twenty-four interpreters, at different stages of their training and professional accreditation, comprising of fifteen Junior Trainee Interpreters (JTI), four Trainee Interpreters (TI), four Members of the Register of Sign Language Interpreters (MRSLI), two Deaf-relay translators (DR), and one DWEB (Deaf Welfare Examination Board accredited, one of the very early routes to qualification) were presented with three texts taken from those that occurred within our initial survey of the types of text that Deaf people present to interpreters, namely: 2011 UK Census, British Gas utility information, and the National Health Service GP patient survey. They were asked to document their thought processes via a Think Aloud Protocol (TAP) within real time (20 minutes), to reflect the timings of appointments currently given to sight translation sessions by some agencies. Within this article a portion of the data collected and analysed will be shown, namely that of an extract of the UK Census 2011 by eight interpreters (2 JTIs, 2 TIs, 2MRSLIs, and 2 DRs).

We grouped their thoughts into ten 'thought' categories: 'domain knowledge and specifics', 'audience', 'vocabulary', 'syntax', 'creativity', 'time and quality boundaries', 'comprehension, re-structure and equivalence', 'justifications and implications', 'legal issues' and 'errors/failures', in part informed by previous sight translation failure studies such as Jiménez Ivars (2008).

Taking the eight candidates together, their thoughts within the ten categories were divided as follows:

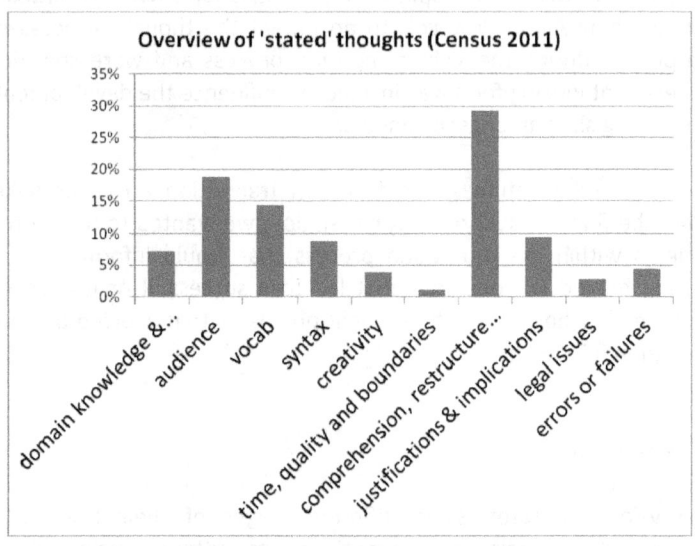

Not surprisingly, the interpreters prioritised their thoughts in the category of 'comprehension, re-structure and equivalence' and dedicated considerable mental energy to this area. It is either the first or second priority of all interpreters. The category of 'audience' also featured highly, being in the top three priorities for all candidates. This could be due to the fact that no Deaf clients were present during the sight translation task performed, though we are of the opinion that sign language interpreters automatically consider the audience, especially in this setting, and have a default position towards this priority.

When we look at the thought distribution amongst each category per candidate (see table below), there was a marked difference between interpreters. Previous studies examining the cognitive processes of more advanced and highly qualified practitioners suggest that they become more automated in their thoughts. Börsch (1986) argues that this also happens when looking at the thoughts of experienced interpreters. Our own data seems to contradict this, as the more qualified interpreters, when taking into account the quantitative measure of cognitive processes, seem to have more thoughts. They do, however, dedicate less mental energy to the category 'vocabulary' which could tentatively suggest a process of automation.

thought categories\candidates	JTI1	JTI2	TI1	TI2	DR1	DR2	MRSLI1	MRSLI2
domain knowledge and specifics	0	0	0	0	1	9	2	1
audience	5	3	1	7	2	6	6	4
vocabulary	2	4	8	1	2	6	0	3
syntax	3	0	0	1	1	1	9	1
creativity	1	1	0	2	1	1	1	0
time and quality boundaries	0	0	0	0	0	0	2	0
comprehension, re-structure and equivalence	5	4	7	5	5	10	10	7
justifications and implications	2	3	0	1	0	1	2	8
legal issues	1	0	0	2	0	1	1	0
errors/failures	0	0	0	0	8	0	0	0

Table1: number of thoughts per category for each candidate

What was revealing is that although each interpreter had their own thought patterns, nevertheless, a common set of thought groups could be identified amongst those still in training and those at a more advanced level. Those still in training did not display thoughts in all of the categories and there was a tendency to focus on the areas of 'comprehension, re-structure and equivalence' and 'vocabulary', accompanied by thoughts in the areas of 'justifications and implications' and the category of 'audience'. The greater emphasis on these categories and in particular on 'justification and implications', we believe, reflects the training philosophy and methods being implemented on their training programme.

The data also showed that some interpreters were predominantly focussing on specific areas; for example, one of the interpreters (TI2) focused for over a third of their thoughts on the 'audience'. Other interpreters focused mainly on the area of 'comprehension, re-structure and equivalence' and the area of 'vocabulary', 94% in the case of one interpreter (TI1). When contrasting an individual's thought allocations with background information available on each candidate, it was found that those interpreters who have greater interaction with the Deaf community, or had Deaf relatives, devoted a larger portion of their thought processes to thinking about the audience. It also allowed us to conclude that those interpreters who mainly work in specific domains, for example, education, focus their thoughts mainly on 'vocabulary', 'comprehension, re-structure and equivalence', in part due to their role and function in that domain, namely, knowledge transfer. Those involved more in community based settings, tended to have an increased number of thoughts in the area of 'syntax' and 'comprehension, re-structure and equivalence', reflecting the diverse language range of their clients whose sign language proficiency was spread across the British Sign Language/English continuum.

The practical use of the analysis of thought processes via TAPs, enables us to determine whether there is an optimum spread of thoughts among the thought categories (safe to practice indicator) and facilitates the identification of specific areas of development for each interpreter, if certain thought categories are absent or under-represented, as it gives an indication within a translation assignment of the possible strengths and weaknesses of the interpreter. The distribution of the thoughts within the thought categories also hints at the role each interpreter was adapting, for example conduit, educator, or advocate.

From undertaking this initial pilot study, we would argue that the early positioning of sight translation within sign language interpreter training, combined with the use of Think Aloud Protocol activities, enhances the rate of growth of interpreters in training. It also builds confidence, reduces anxiety levels, and allows trainee interpreters to become more autonomous. The use of TAPs within sight translation training was in particular instrumental and highly beneficial for trainees (JTI/TI) when commencing the task of learning how to interpret, especially from English to BSL. We observed that it shifted their cognitive processes away from searching for equivalence at a word level (category 'vocabulary'), and promoted their thinking towards the broader conceptual level (category 'comprehension, re-structure and equivalence'). The introduction of TAPs within the weekly sessions of the *Introduction to Interpreting Issues* module, supported via tutor led online individual and group blogs, resulted in a rapid acceleration of their mental energy being assigned to priority categories. Their interpreting abilities became underpinned by an increased self-assurance in their accurate use and manipulation of their first and second language.

5. Conclusions

In conclusion, the use of TAPs, and the subsequent analysis into thought categories, allowed us as trainers to directly intervene by identifying areas of development and fine tuning further sessions to meet the individual needs of those in training, in the specific areas where necessary, and discern areas of continuing professional development for those who were already practitioners. This points to the introduction of TAPs within the learning process as a positive solution in making the training of sight translation more effective. We would argue that just as the inclusion of sight translation is paramount to interpreter training, *"...mastering the skills involved in this complex textual reformulation process is a must for those seeking for qualification and insertion in the professional milieu of translators and interpreters..."* (Sampaio 2007:68), so should TAPs be regarded as an essential part of the training process of sight translation itself. One could even go as far as to propose that the engagement with TAPs ought to have added benefits in relation to the training of other modes of interpreting.

References

Agrifoglio M. 2004. Sight Translation and interpreting: a comparative analysis of constraints and failures, *Interpreting* 6:1, 43-67 Amsterdam: John Benjamins Publishing Company.

Biela-Wolońclej A. 2007. A-VISTA: new challenges for tailor-made translation types on the example of recorded sight translation, *Kalbotyra* 57:3, 30-39.

Börsch S. 1986. Introspective methods in research on interlingual and intercultural communication. In J. House and S. Blum-Kulka (eds), *Interlingual and Intercultural communication. Discourse and Cognition in Translation and Second Language Acquisition Studies*. Tübingen: Gunter Narr, 195-209.

Curvers P., J. Klein, N. Riva and C. Wuilmart 1986. La traduction á vue comme exercice préparatoire et complémentaire á l'interprétation de conférence. *Cuadernos de Traducció e Interpretació* 7, 97-116.

Dragsted B. and I. Hansen 2009. Exploring translation and interpreting Hybrids. The case of sight translation, *Meta Translators' Journal* LIV:3, 588-604.

Falbo C. 1995. Interprétation consécutive et exercices préparatoires. *The Interpreters' Newsletter* 6, 87-91.

Gile D. 1985. Le modèle d'efforts et l'equilibre en interprétation simultanée. *Meta* 30:1, 44-8.

Gile D. 1995. *Basic concepts and models for interpreters and translator training.* Amsterdam: John Benjamins Publishing Company.

Gile D. 2002. Conference interpreting as a cognitive management problem. In F. Pöchhacker and M. Shlesinger (eds), *The Interpreting Studies Reader.* London: Routledge, 162-176.

Jiménez Ivars A. 2008. Sight translation and written translation. A comparative analysis of causes of problems, strategies and translation errors within the PACTE translation competence model, *Internacional científic* 6:2, 79-104.

Kim C. 2001. *Sight Translation in its own right.* Master's Degree Dissertation. Monterey Bay: California State University.

Kovačič I. 1997. A Thinking-aloud experiment in subtitling. In M. Snell-Hornby, Z. Jettmarová and K. Kaindl (eds), *Translation as Intercultural Communication. Selected papers from the EST Congress, Prague 1995*, Amsterdam: John Benjamins, 229-238.

Lambert S. 2004. Shared attention during sight translation, sight interpretation and simultaneous interpretation, *Meta: journal des traducteurs,* 49:2, 294-306.

Martin A. 1993. Teaching sight translation to future interpreters. In C. Picken (ed), *XIII World Congress of FIT Translation-the vital link 6-13 Aug 1993 Brighton,* London: Institute of Translation and Interpreting, Volume 1, 398-405.

Pochhäcker F. 2004. *Introducing Interpreting Studies,* London: Routledge.

Pöchhacker F. and M. Shlesinger (eds.) 2002. *The Interpreting Studies Reader*. London: Routledge.

Sampaio G.R.L. 2007. Mastering sight translation skills, *Tradução & Comunicação* 16, 63-69.

Sofer M. 2006. *The Translator's Handbook*, 6th revised edition, Rockville: Schreiber Publishing.

Viaggio S. 1995. The praise of sight translation (and squeezing the last drop thereout of), *The Interpreters' Newsletter* 6, 33-42.

Viezzi M. 1989a. Information retention as a parameter for the comparison of sight translation and simultaneous interpretation: An experimental study. *The Interpreters' Newsletter* 2, 65–69.

Viezzi M. 1989b. Sight translation: An experimental analysis. In J. Dodds (ed), *Aspects of English: Miscellaneous papers for English teachers and specialists*. Udine: Campanotto, 109–140.

Viezzi M. 1990. Sight translation, simultaneous interpretation and information retention. In L. Gran and C. Taylor (eds), *Aspects of applied and experimental research on conference interpretation*. Udine: Campanotto, 54–60.

Weber W. 1990. The importance of sight translation in an interpreter training program. In D. Bowen and M. Bowen (eds), *Interpreting – Yesterday, Today and Tomorrow*. Binghamton: State University of New York, 44-52.

Translating poetry

Valeria Buonomo and Pietro Celo

1. Introduction

We feel that the theme of efsli 2011 is rather avant-garde with respect to the professional scene in Italy, where so-called 'sight translation', or the way of translating written language into sign language and vice versa, is still not used very much in both informal (negotiations) and formal (conferences, for example) work contexts. Perhaps the contrary direction, from sign language to written language, is starting to be in greater demand (consider, for example, cases in which a deaf person asks to have his or her thesis translated in written form or cases in which a film on DVD has to be translated with correct subtitles).

When in 2009, together with our students of interpretation, we decided to go into greater depth in our textual analysis of several twentieth century Italian poems, we found that we were working according to the former of the two abovementioned ways of translating, that is, written language towards sign language (Celo 2009).

Before engaging in the analysis of the poem we chose for this paper, we first define the presupposition that inspired us to translate it.

2. On translating poetry

Translating literary texts like poetry into sign language, which is usually considered a *difficult* if not *impossible* task, is not really any different than translating any other written text (whatever genre it be: narrative, descriptive, expository, etc.) and, to go even further, it is not even very different from translating any other kind of oral text of vocal language. The difficulties encountered are great in any event. In fact, when we speak of translation *from* a vocal language (both oral and written) *into* a sign language and vice versa, we are referring to an *interlinguistic* translation (that is, a true 'translation' between two languages); at the same time, we are also (if not above all) referring to an *intersemiotic* translation. That is, we are talking about a translation, an operation that almost reaches the limits of the untranslatable, where we sign language

35

interpreters can only grope around in our search for an interpretarial passage that is at least decent, or one that can institute the conditions, however minimal they might be, for textual equivalence ('equivalence of value', the primary objective of a good translation) between the text in the 'language for hearers' and the one in the 'language for the deaf'.

Thus, when we speak of translation *from* and *into* sign language, and if we are speaking of it with an awareness of cause, that is, seeing it as an *intersemiotic* translation, we are still in fact talking about a 'hard' if not 'impossible' translation – whether it is a case of a translation of oral texts in everyday language, or a translation of more complex written texts, as is the case with the poetic text we will deal with here.

Essentially, we are trying to say that *intersemiotic* translation is an inevitable theme if we truly want to talk about translation between 'language for hearers' and 'language for the deaf', and the case that we will put forward here is a further occasion to reaffirm the special quality and complexity of this intersemiotic translation process.

3. Notes on the special quality of intersemiotic translation

Intersemiotic translation was defined by the linguist R. Jakobson (1966), who used the term with reference to translation from and to vocal languages and nonverbal languages (such as music, dance, film, etc.).

In 2010, we felt the need to give it a new meaning by referring to translation to and from vocal languages and sign languages, referring to common translating and interpreting procedures, and we published this research in a hitherto non-existent text in our profession, *L'interprete di lingua dei segni* (Buonomo and Celo 2010). In this text, we move from Jakobson's distinction between the forms of translation and from his idea of a third form (intersemiotic translation) to introduce – perhaps for the first time – a specific, particular idea in the field of interpreting of a twofold translation between vocal languages and sign languages: partly interlinguistic and highly intersemiotic:

> We must underline that if until the present time intersemiotic translation, starting with scholars of semiotics and the theory of language, has been taken into consideration in the relation between a system of

linguistic signs and another of non-linguistic signs, perhaps it would be worth dedicating some attention to this intersemiotic dimension in the case of an interpretarial process between two semiotic systems – both linguistic, of course, but where the continual change of sensorial channel forces the Interpreter of sign language to the following passages. In fact, he/she is forced, on the one hand, to never lose sight of the morpho-syntactic aspects of linguistic linearity (in vocal language as well as in sign language), but on the other, he/she must account for the transformation of what is born as linear and sequential (discrete), and that cannot assume cinematic or multi-modal form (continual) in the case of voice-Sign translation. This twofold nature of the interpretarial process already originates in the corresponding twofold nature of sign language: linear and sequential, and thus discrete, on a par with every other linguistic system that pertains to the organ of hearing, but at the same time cinematic and multi-modal, thus continuous, on a par with every other semiotic system that pertains to the organ of sight (Buonomo and Celo 2010: 50).

Intersemiotic translation (always together with the interlinguistic translation aspect) is the only possible form of translation among languages which do not share the same linguistic expressive level (as in Hjelmslev 1968), that is, the same "expression channel": vocal-written, thus linear for one language, and manual-oral, thus not only linear but also multi-modal and continual for the other.

The special quality of *intersemiotic* translation is due to the following properties:

- *it is not simply a transcoding procedure*, that is, where source and target texts are mapped onto each other one by one (as happens with Braille, for example);

- *it is not simply an interlinguistic translation*, as when we are faced with two 'languages for hearers' who share the same sensorial channel they communicate in. The channel forces upon them a rather similar process of awareness and re-signification of the world, thus making them 'close to each other', so to speak, and as a consequence, highly translatable.[1]

The special form of *intersemiotic* translation is due to the following properties:

- *it is a complex form of transcultural action*, that is, a translation on the edge between two different ways of living from an ontological viewpoint (being deaf is not like being able to hear, and vice versa), with consequences on the linguistic plane as well: the codified meanings in sign language are very far from being diversified by sectors, genres and specific contexts as happens in vocal languages, and are thus very far from being equal (in the sense of practice) with respect to such an imposing written tradition in vocal languages. In fact, at the present state of the art, translating into sign language involves peripeteia, and sometimes 'using one's imagination' to translate everything that can be said or written in the 'language for hearers';

- *it involves a dynamic, complex form of action*, or a translation on the edge between the need to be coherent to the text and the need to transform it into a different level of expression, for example a film based on a written novel, by its very nature (different from the source text), it must adapt its dynamic forms to the linear form of the source text and in this way it moves away from it per force, becoming something completely different on the level of expression, while on the level of content the challenge of possible translatability remains open. Essentially, it is above all on the level of expression that intersemiotic translation often meets with difficulties and is thus forced to make some courageous choices.[2] On the level of content, intersemiotic translation shows its more dynamic and (why not?) *creative* aspect, perhaps accepting to be only a partial translation, or to prune or polish the source text where it considers it necessary, or to shift to a certain textual

---

[1] For a broad, well-articulated survey of that exemplifies concrete cases of intersemiotic translation, although without any reference to sign languages, see Dusi and Nergaard (2001).

[2] In our own words, 'azzardi interpretariali' like, for example, the production of a manual classifier as linguistic performer with the purpose of evoking a meaning that is as close as possible to the source word, or like the expansion of the meaning of a sign through an emphatic use of the labializiation that conforms to the vocal word despite the fact that the sign is more commonly associated with a different labialization (see Buonomo and Celo 2010).

level when it encounters zones of untranslatability, that is, selecting the levels of content to be translates into the target language (for example, isolating and thus translating only the narrative level of sequences and giving up on the translation of stylistic aspects, or vice versa).

Despite this separation of the level of expression from that of content, we should bear in mind that in every language (whether vocal or sign), the two levels do not and cannot live separately, but are rather linked by 'mutual solidarity' (Hjemslev 1968), or by ties of interrelation and interdependence. Therefore, translating consists in re-activating and selecting the system of relations between the two levels in the source text and in the target text, and to translate, that is, to transfer these relationships adequately into the target language (Torop 1995/2000) – in other words: to always translate the statement, but also to always translate the enunciation, or better, it's possible strategies (Meschonnic 1973, 1990, 1999).

We conclude this introduction to what we think is the priority form of translation from and into sign language (without forgetting interlinguistic translation), inasmuch as it is intersemiotic translation. Through this form of translation, we will analyse the decisions made in translating the poetic text under examination here, thus keeping the multi-sensorial tension of the translation alive in its dynamic complexity, like a journey which always hangs in balance between these two different languages, 'for hearers' and 'for the deaf', in that they are very far apart, but always translatable ... we just have to translate that distance.

4. Approach to the poetic text

Even if, as we have seen, intersemiotic translation is always difficult – if not at the limits of the impossible – whether a poetic text is involved or not, it is also true that poetry involves no less adventurous challenges that must be taken up with courage and a little artistic license. Bringing out this passion, accompanying the reader as far as possible into these areas, is difficult and complex to aim for, and we would like to share this in the present paper.

In a good translation, the dilemma between maintaining loyalty to the original text and saving artistic beauty need not lead one astray. In fact, it is not possible simply to translate the text alone without risking an arid superimposition of forms and meanings, nor can we all be poets capable of translating the work of other poets, or have a literary soul and knowledge of literature. Nevertheless, it is also not possible simply to base the translation solely on the knowledge of the context alone, whether this be linguistic, geographical, social, or cultural. Whatever the context may be – linguistic or non-linguistic, knowledge of it does not solve the translating-interpreting problem of the literary text. Such an approach, which calls upon the context, can end up parcelling out the translation as it is done and constructed, thus deciding what is legitimate or not in the act of translation or interpreting, and is therefore misleading.

In accordance with traditional rules for translating, we can borrow a foreign word or expression, which we can use as an imprint, and then transpose or modulate it into another language, or we can translate with a cultural equivalence or, in the spirit of a good translation, with an adaptation. This approach may be considered as legitimate, generally speaking, but it neglects the literary aspect of translation. The problems of how to render the poetic spirit and meaning (or rather the poetic "intention" of the author) and how to avoid abuse of the literary text are not solved. In attempting to be poets ourselves, we run the risk of creating a free adaptation of the text at hand and not a genuine translation. Thus, a more complex view of this topic, which takes into account the formal and literary part of the poem, the context of the author's message and the spirit (why not?) of the translator allows us to approach the problem of translation that we are concerned with.

As stated above, only recently were we given the opportunity to say that in cases of translation *from* and *into* sign language, we are dealing with translation between languages of equal dignity, but also – and above all – intersemiotic or transmodal translation, where faithfulness to the source text has specific meanings that assume particular, complex meanings. For example, it is difficult to imagine a lexical correspondence between a language like Italian, with its rich literary tradition, grammatical stability, and important written noble part, and a language like Italian sign language, where the "signer" is a grammatical part of the language itself, the rule in space and a constituent part. Only recently has it knowingly made moves in the literary direction, and for that matter exclusively oral.

Thus, in our case, faithfulness to the concept of *poetic musicality*, dear to certain translations, takes on uncertain and undefined outlines, and thus, having excluded grammatical, semantic, phraseological and phonetic faithfulness to the text for structural reasons (diversity on the level of expression), we are left with faithfulness to the poem itself. We can identify its aims and its means, in its deep meaning and structure.

We decided to work intensely with understanding the original, profound sense of the source text, aware that any translation must aim for that. Understanding the original meaning helped us to find the means of restoring it to sign language through so-called 'non-manual components', which in our case turned out to be the linguistic elements essential to translate the pragmatic subtleties of the poetic text – not the words or grammar, but the tone, the feeling, or the profound *sense* of the poetic text. And in this way, in the phase of studying the text, in this experience of pre-translation, we approached the text, the poet and the context to understand the meaning of the poem. We have reflected, chosen independently and loved our text for its similar temperament and conception of the world we have seen there, but we have also hated it for its difficulties, for the remoteness of its emotions or correspondence with our soul. We are not poets, but interpreters, perhaps poetic ones. It seems like proceeding by fragments, seeking Croce's beautiful verse (*il bel verso*) – or better beautiful translation (*la bella traduzione*) – perhaps carried out almost by chance. But this is not the case, and we will try to demonstrate it through a detailed analysis of Primo Levi's poem, *Se questo è un uomo*, which attracted us for its strength and its warning which, like a scream, we like to think has not been lost in translation.

5. A short biography of Primo Levi

Primo Levi (Turin, 31 July 1919 - 11 April 1987) was an Italian writer author of memoirs, tales, lyrics and novels. In 1934, he entered the Massimo d'Azeglio Royal Gymnasium in Turin, famous for its illustrious teachers and young students, who later became anti-Fascists, like Augusto Monti, Franco Antonicelli, Umberto Cosmo, Zino Zini, Norberto Bobbio, Fernanda Pivano and many others. Cesare Pavese was his Italian teacher for a few months.

He graduated from the school in 1937 and enrolled in the chemistry programme at the University of Turin. September 1938 marks the introduction of racial laws which prohibited Jewish people to study unless they were already enrolled. Luckily, Primo Levi was already in his second year of studies. However, racial laws indirectly (but decisively) influenced his intellectual and university career. In fact, he realized that he loved physics more than chemistry, and he changed universities. Unfortunately, he was a Jew and only had the option of finishing the programme he had already started. Later, although he had taken all his exams on time, he could not find a reader for his final thesis. Yet he managed to get his degree, with excellence and merit, in 1941, presenting a thesis in physics. On his certificate, «of the Jewish race» is written.

The racial laws of the Fascist regime also influenced his life after university, forcing him to take occasional jobs because he was a Jew.

In 1943, after a short time of collaboration with the partisans, he was arrested by the Fascist militia in Brusson (AO) and taken in the concentration camp in Fossoli.

In February 1944, he was handed over by the Italians to the Nazis and deported as a "Häftling"(literally, "prisoner") to Auschwitz (in the camp Auschwitz III - Monowitz with the number 174517). After first being sentenced to forced labour, he started working in the chemistry laboratories of Buna, a synthetic rubber manufacturer. He fell ill with scarlet fever, and then succeeded in avoiding the evacuation march in Auschwitz just before the liberation of the camp by the Red Army.

He was set free on 27 January 1945, even though his journey back took place only in the following October. When he returned to Turin, he found a job in a paint firm. Shortly thereafter, he became director of this firm until he retired. After that, he dedicated more and more time to his novels.

His dramatic experience in the Nazi Lager inspired *Se questo è un uomo* (*If This is a Man*), which tells about his time in prison. It has been translated into many languages, including German. *I sommersi e i salvati*, a novel, came out decades later. He tries to analyse his experience from a distance, comparing the Nazi universe in the Lager with other similar ones, for example the Soviet world as described in the writings of

Aleksandr Solzhenitsyn, and trying to find common elements and differences. In Italy at that time, after the reconstruction after the War, nobody felt like thinking about the horror it had caused, and so in 1937, the publisher Einaudi did not want to publish Levi's work. But De Silva agreed to print 2,500 copies, and succeeded in selling 1,500 mainly in Turin, perhaps due to the very good review by Italo Calvino in the newspaper *Unità*.

It was not until the Sixties that Levi came to be considered an important writer. His *La tregua* was based on the memories of his adventurous journey back to Italy. It is a sort of travel journal through devastated post-War Europe. When he got back to Turin he felt the burning need to go on telling and writing, to describe the indescribable, to let himself as a man tell other men what mankind was capable of doing. So he wrote the novels *La chiave a stella* and *Se non ora, quando?*, as well as the collection of short stories *Il sistema periodico*. On April 11, 1987, Levi was found at the bottom of the staircase in his home in Turin; a possible suicide is suspected.

Claudio Toscani said about him: "Primo Levi's last message does not say do not forget me, but rather do not forget." In 1997, ten years after his death, the film director Francesco Rosi paid tribute to his memory by making a film based on the novel *La tregua*. The leading actor was John Turturro.

6. The Shemà

Published in 1947, *Se questo è un uomo* is a historic document as well as a personal testimonial. It is now recognized as a classic in the literature dedicated to the atrocious memories of Nazism. The author writes in a dramatic, but strong and effective way about his terrible experience in the concentration camp, giving us a shocking picture of the horrors and suffering. It is not a tragic lament, but an invitation to know about, meditate on and elaborate strategies (internal and external) so that in the history of man and the conditions that permitted the birth and rise of an ideology like Nazism will not happen again.

The title of the work also refers to the need *not to forget* the atrocious demolition of human dignity, and so does the poem at the beginning of the novel, which defines the theme and justifies its title. The poem is inspired by the form of the 'Shemà', one of the most intimate, deeply felt Jewish prayers. It is like a paraphrase, a prayer that should be said twice a day, morning and evening.

The Shemà has an introduction with two verses, and three parts, made up of passages from the Torah. Originally the Shemà contained important precepts for Jewish life: total devotion to faith, compulsory education with a lifelong learning value, the prohibition of idolatry, duty to respect *mizvot*, positive or negative commandments, obligations and prohibitions. All of this is enriched and made more profound by the repetition and power of the rule: *...and you will put these words I give you as an order today in your heart, you will teach them to your children, you will say them while having a rest at home, while walking in the street, when you wake up and every time you get up in the morning.* The Shemà also has some warnings about the respect of the commandments from God and the punishments he gives to those who do not respect them, so that the responsibility will be collective and not only individual.

In Jewish families, the father teaches children the Shemà as soon as they are able to talk and write. If you ask any Jewish person what their main prayer is, few will not answer that the Shemà is. They all know it by heart and say it (as in the Shemà itself) "every time they go to sleep and when they get up in the morning."

Primo Levi paraphrased the Shemà by adding some typical motifs and stylistic elements taken from the Jewish prayer: the obligation of being constant in respecting the precept, the obligation of knowing the prayer by heart and accepting punishment for not respecting it or recognizing how serious a crime it is to deny its precepts.

7. Analysis of the poem 'Se questo è un uomo'

Voi che vivete sicuri
Nelle vostre tiepide case,
Voi che trovate tornando a sera
Il cibo caldo e visi amici:
Considerate se questo è un uomo
Che lavora nel fango
Che non conosce pace
Che lotta per mezzo pane

Che muore per un sì o per un no.
Considerate se questa è una donna,
Senza capelli e senza nome
Senza più forza di ricordare
Vuoti gli occhi e freddo il grembo
Come una rana d'inverno
Meditate che questo è stato:
Vi comando queste parole.
Scolpitele nel vostro cuore
Stando in casa andando per via,
Coricandovi alzandovi;
Ripetetele ai vostri figli.
O vi si sfaccia la casa,
La malattia vi impedisca,
I vostri nati torcano il viso da voi.

English translation:

You who live safe
In your warm houses,
You who find warm food
And friendly faces
when you return home.
Consider if this is a man
Who works in mud,
Who knows no peace,
Who fights for a crust of bread,
Who dies by a yes or a no.
Consider if this is a woman
Without hair, without name,
Without the strength to remember,
Empty are her eyes, cold her womb,
Like a frog in winter.
Never forget that this has happened.
Remember these words.
Engrave them in your hearts,
When at home or in the street,
When lying down, when getting up.
Repeat them to your children
Or may your houses be destroyed,
May illness strike you down,

May your offspring turn their faces from you.

In this poem, Levi first shows us something like a family atmosphere, the description of a normal family routine, and it is everyday people who live ordinary lives that the author addresses, with an invitation to think. People living in "human" conditions have warm houses and hot meals to come back to at night after work, and they meet their familiar faces (*tiepide* "warm" refers to human warmth).

In the second strophe, he describes the opposite situation of life in the concentration camps. Levi wants people to think about it, to ask themselves whether someone who works in the mud all day without resting, and with no way of finding peace for even a single moment can possibly be a man.

The author's reflections go even deeper when looking at the conditions of the women who were deported, who were deprived of their names and lost the will to live because they knew they were going to die. Levi is not talking about one man in particular, but of an entire category of people, the Jews, persecuted by the Nazis. The most outstanding part of the poem is the third, where Levi asks us to think about everything that happened and entreats us not to forget. For those who supported racist ideas, Levi sends a curse upon them: their homes should be destroyed, their bodies should be wracked by illnesses, and their children should abandon them forever.

After understanding the context and having gone into depth in the text to search for the profound meaning of this poem, of this prayer, it may be worthwhile to look at the specific translating problems that we gave priority to in translating this poem into Italian sign language.[3]

Voi che vivete sicuri
Nelle vostre tiepide case,
Voi che trovate tornando a sera
Il cibo caldo e visi amici:
In the poem *sicuri* "safe", *tiepide* and *caldo* "warm" are attributes that convey tranquillity, the emotional warmth of the hearth and home. In sign language, the signs for WARM and STEAMING HOT food are in

---

[3] For the translation into Italian sign language, see Celo (2009).

handshape rhyme. Moreover, HUG expresses the sense of intimacy in this situation.

Considerate se questo è un uomo
The word *considerare* "consider" is something more than just 'think about' or 'reflect upon'. It also means to gaze at something, like when you look at the sky or the stars – at the *sidera* (con-sidera) the constellations, hence destiny, divinity – to observe the heavens in order to deeply understand all the things that we humans can barely see since our sight has limits for distance. In the translation, the repetition of the verb TO THINK, emphasized symmetrically by using both hands, adds something, thus giving a more intense form of 'think'.

Che lavora nel fango
Che non conosce pace
In the poem, the word *pace* "peace" means 'inner peace'. In the sign language translation, the sign for PEACE is produced in the usual neutral space, but it is followed by the sign INSIDE, on the body, to mean 'inner peace'.

Che lotta per mezzo pane
Besides the singular relevance of *crust of bread* in the English translation, the value of the word *mezzo* "half" when associated with *pane* "bread" is interesting, because it takes on a negative value that to a certain extent evokes desperation: 'half' in the sense of not whole, something that is not worth the whole. In the translation into sign language, *mezzo pane* was rendered with 'PART of a piece of bread' with the use of a classifier that is very effective in expressing the smallness of *that* piece of bread.

Che muore per un sì o per un no.
Here the translation is creative in taking up the image of the gesture of condemnation or redemption, with the thumb up or down, as the ancient Romans did after battles in the arena.

Considerate se questa è una donna,
Senza capelli e senza nome
Senza più forza di ricordare
In the poem *senza capelli* "without hair" is a simple negation, referring to the absence of hair, without a *before* or an *after*; instead, in the sign language translation, the word for RASATI "SHAVED" was chosen.

Moreover, following the nature of intersemiotic translation for an audience that listens with their eyes and is moved thereby, it was decided not to leave the value *e senza nome* "without name" out, but to make it clear with the translation NUMBER TATOOED ON HER ARM, exactly as happened in the concentration camps, thus strengthening the value of depersonalization and reification of man. In sign language, this meaning has already found its expression in the classifier 5#, to be represented in space symmetrically and with MAN and WOMAN opposed to each other already at the 4th line.

Vuoti gli occhi e freddo il grembo
Come una rana d'inverno
Meditate che questo è stato:
The meaning of the word *meditare* "meditate" is both measure and think, to measure with the mind in a repetitive and accurate way – we could say 'analyse', as the very scientific Levi himself would. In the translation, the rhyme found in Italian (with the verb PENS<u>ARE</u> (THINK) corresponding to 'consider<u>are</u>' (consider) of lines 5 and 10) is also rendered.

Vi comando queste parole.
Scolpitele nel vostro cuore
The intensity of *vi comando* (in English translated with the imperative form of the verb), translated with I ORDER YOU, is followed by a strong image *scolpitele nel vostro cuore* "engrave them in your hearts", meaning *ricordatele* "remember them" as well as CONSERVATELE IN MEMORIA "KEEP THEM IN MEMORY", as is translated in sign language, an almost physical memory that is *scolpita* "engraved or carved" just as stone is (as can be seen in the translation: SCOLPIRE-PIETRA "CARVE/ENGRAVE-STONE" and "CARVE/ENGRAVE-HEART").

Stando in casa andando per via,
Coricandovi alzandovi;
As required by the Shemà, the ritual invocation is rendered in the translation by the increasing rhythm of the sign language and by the symmetric use of the space around the sign language translator.

Ripetetele ai vostri figli.
In the poem, *ripetetele* "repeat them" is translated into sign language as RACCONTATE "TELL", where the salient quality of the repetition is given through the reiteration of the sign.

O vi si sfaccia la casa,
The choice of the privative *s-* in Italian *sfaccia*, which is also difficult to translate with other vocal languages, is intense. The translation hence stops at the most easily comprehensible equivalent DESTROY (*vi si distrugga la casa* "may your houses be destroyed").

La malattia vi impedisca,
That is, "may it put something between your feet" (*in-pedibus*), 'limit you' or 'just barely let you live', is rendered in translation with SPREAD IN YOUR MIDST, or 'enter into you' exactly as a virus might 'enter' your body.

I vostri nati torcano il viso da voi.
That is your 'your lineage, your offspring' but in the word *nati* "born" it is almost impossible to obtain the same dignity as the word *figli* "sons, children" – this remains in the grey area of indefiniteness, anonymity, without placing the accent on family relationships. In the translation into sign language, the sign for FIGLIO "SON/CHILD", where the singular reinforces the sense of anonymity, accentuating the facial expression of negativity that foreshadows the next phrase 'turn their faces from you', rendered in sign language not only with signs but also through an almost chilling impersonation where the eyes of the CHILD intentionally move away from the place of 'you (plural)' with the sign GUARDARE "LOOK", performed with the gesture of covering the face of the one who must not be looked at ('plural you', in fact) and the impersonation of the eyes that remain frozen in the void, in a neutral space where the 'you (plural)' that the poet is referring to is not planned for.

In conclusion, the search for the meaning, the author's intention, the context of his experience and the words he left all cooperated with the translator to create, metaphorically speaking, a sort of parallel text – a kind of metaphorical, comparative text, which has the acoustic essence of the music of a vinyl LP, which makes the lines and flaws of sound vibrant, and almost allows us to see the fingers strumming the guitar, giving us genuine emotions. It is a way of observing to what extent the expression lines on our forehead restore the profound meaning of this poem to us.

References

Buonomo V. and P. Celo 2010. *L'Interprete di lingua dei segni italiana. Problemi linguistici, aspetti emotivi, formazione Professionale*. Milano: Ed. Hoepli.

Celo P. (ed.) 2009. *I segni del '900. Poesie italiane del Novecento tradotte nella lingua dei segni italiana. Con DVD*. Venezia: Ed. Cafoscarina.

Dusi N. and S. Nergaard (eds) 2000. "Sulla intersemiotic translation". *Versus. Quaderni di studi semiotica* (85/86/87).

Hjelmslev L. 1968. *I fondamenti della teoria del linguaggio* [1961]. Torino: Einaudi.

Jakobson R. 1966. Aspetti linguistici della translation [1958]. In *Saggi di linguistica generale* [1963]. Milano: Feltrinelli, 56-64).

Meschonnic A. 1973. *Pour la poétique* [1970]. Paris: Gallimard.

Meschonnic A. 1990. *La rime et la vie*. Lagrasse: Verdier.

Meschonnic A. 1999. *Poétique du traduire*. Lagrasse: Verdier.

Torop P. 1995. *Total'nyj perevod* [La traduzione totale]. Tartu, Tartu Ülikooli Kirjastus [Edizioni dell'Università di Tartu]. Trad. italiana *La traduzione totale*, a cura di B. Osimo, Modena, Logos-Guaraldi, 2000.

Sight translation with meaning in a signing world
Sharon Neumann Solow

1. Introduction

For those approaching a task in sight translation – or any form of translation, *meaning* is the central consideration: maintaining the meaning of the source material, and conveying that meaning accurately and clearly to the client. After all, why are you there in the first place if not to convey meaning? It is critical that we provide actual service. Unfortunately, when we are interpreting, even when we are doing a completely ineffective job, there is the appearance of service. The interpreter may be the only one who knows if the work is more or less effective.

Sometimes sight translation interpreters forget to check for *meaning* because they become so involved in the printed text and focus on words only. Despite this very real temptation, our focus must remain on the accurate and complete transfer of meaning. Intrusion from the source text language easily occurs when we are reading the words and signing them to a client.

Another difficulty when we translate directly from written texts is that there is sometimes a lack of natural language processing and prosody In the rendering of sight translations. Again, if we hold the transfer of meaning as the most important thing we do, then we will remain deliberate and conscious of our effect; doing so improves our work in sight translation so that we produce more natural interpretations that carry appropriate prosody so that the clients' accurate comprehension is more likely.

Furthermore, some Sign Language interpreters have limited or no formal training in sight translation. Some also do not have a great deal of experience in doing sight translation. For these and many other reasons, it is extremely important that efsli has taken up this topic for its 2011 annual conference.

2. Signed sight translation vs. spoken language sight translation

The work of sight translators has much in common with that of spoken language interpreters, but there are also significant differences to consider. I will mention two here.

1. Physical position relative to client: Whereas spoken language interpreters typically do sight translation looking over the client's shoulder (or sitting next to the client and reading aloud, without looking at him or her very often), we look directly at the deaf party a great deal of the time as we interpret. It may be easier for a spoken language interpreter to render difficult or discomfiting information because the interpreter is not looking right at the client's face. By contrast, signed sight translators sit face-to-face with our clients, making frequent eye contact, throughout the interpretation. This more "intimate" position relative to the client challenges our ability to maintain an appearance of neutrality when the content of the interpretation gives rise to feelings of sympathy, anger, disgust or any other personal responses we might have to the material itself, and/or to the clients' reactions to that material. However, if we are steeled for this – prepared and conscious – we can maintain proper distance and professionalism, and tend to the objective of conveying *meaning*. I observed a colleague doing a sight translation of extremely difficult and tragic information. Her sympathy was evident, giving a strong sense of bias or non-impartiality. I believe she was unaware of her affect. Awareness is the first step. If we realize the danger we are better prepared to avoid it.

2. Privacy: Another intriguing difference between sight translation and spoken language translation is that, in situations in which confidentiality is a concern, spoken language interpreters must ensure that their work is not *overheard*, whereas sight translators must be certain that we are not seen. A sight translation can be visible from some distance. Anyone in the vicinity who understands sign language could have access to confidential information. We always must check the environment and establish ourselves in the most secure location for the privacy of the client.

3. Advantages inherent in sight translation (for the interpreter)

Often the sight translation material we are given is quite complex. In these cases, in particular, it is essential to scan the document in order to gain a sense of the overall point, goals and content of the printed matter to be sight translated. (This is one of the many benefits of sight translation; we typically have an opportunity to become familiar in advance with the content of the entire document to be interpreted.)

In sight translating a document, the interpreter has control over the material, including the ability to reread material and/or refer back to earlier segments of the document. These are luxuries we don't normally have in interpretation of spoken and signed texts.

Access to the entire source text allows discourse level analysis and restructuring in advance of the sight translation with the client. In addition, Deaf Interpreters can access the written form without a relay pivot interpreter (hearing interpreter).

Text analysis can increase the interpreter's efficiency in preparing for the sight translation task. It is important to assess the level of complexity and the context in which this document is being read, as well as the purpose or goal of the communicative event: Is it intended to stimulate, inform, entertain, actuate, convince or persuade? In assessing the content of the source text, the interpreter can determine the topic, its complexity and familiarity to the client and to the interpreter him/herself and in what way this document or these documents will be or are related to the interpreting assignment in which they occur and to what has already transpired. The interpreter also has an opportunity to determine the density of the material and to watch for culturally and linguistically challenging aspects, such as sound-based content or puns in a printed text. The complexity of a text may be due to language issues, lexical, phrasal, sentential or syntactic elements, discourse level issues or cultural differences.

Whole thought processing is an essential component in sight translation for meaning. We begin by reading enough to understand before rendering a sight translation. We work in whole thoughts, which requires that we begin and end every thought before moving on to the next. This is well-supported by the deliberate, appropriate and attentive use of cohesion and transition markers. Natural Articulation is a happy result of whole thought processing. Appropriate prosody and accurate grammatical choices are more likely in a well-processed sight translation with a focus on meaning and on working at the level of whole thoughts.

Sight translation can be a completely *consecutive process*, allowing more time and more opportunities for appropriate target language discourse structuring than are available in simultaneous or consecutive interpretation, because the interpreter can often control the amount of time spent on the task.

The *intimacy* of the sight translation situation – and the absence of other individuals in this setting – may prompt the client to invite the interpreter to chat. While this has the potential to pose some challenges, it also may be an advantage. It may offer an opportunity for the translator to become familiar with the client's language, dialect and style for the upcoming face-to-face interpretation.

4. Strategies for maximizing accuracy and effectiveness in sight translation

Sight translation presents many challenges but several strategies and techniques can help the interpreter be more effective.

1. Awareness: We need to look at our work and our approach to the work regularly to maintain a conscious and deliberate practice. Awareness is a highly effective tool in improving our approach to the work, and the work itself.

2. Reading Comprehension and Speed: Reading comprehension and speed aid efficient sight translation. Quite obviously, excellent reading comprehension is a critical skill interpreters must possess. Reading speed is essential so that the sight translation effort does not take too long and so that the interpreter can get as much information quickly in as efficient a manner as possible.

3. Scanning and Skimming Skills: An interpreter must scan for content and style while analysing units of meaning and anticipating syntactic rearrangement to be rendered in the target language. Skimming is another helpful strategy in preparing effective sight translations; this might take the form of reading the first and last paragraphs of a

document or of each section of a document and the first and last sentence in each paragraph in advance of rendering the sight translation.

4. Semantic Accuracy, Jargon and Lexical/Syntactic Considerations: In order to understand enough to create a meaningful sight translation, it is important to look up or ask about challenging lexical items such as technical terms or jargon. Semantic accuracy requires attentive processing at every level. At the lexical level, it is important to read for meaning and not be seduced by simple sign-for-word behaviours. For example, a sentence like *Has a history of ear infections* might be translated as "UP-TO-NOW EAR I-N-F-E-C-T-I-O-N POP-UP OCCASIONAL"; note that it is not likely that the ASL sign for "HISTORY" would be used at all in this context. The interpreter can also check, confirm and remember the proper spelling of lexical items in the source text. At the syntactic level, the interpreter has the opportunity to restructure grammatical units that are especially difficult such as passive in English or rhetorical questions in ASL, thus avoiding intrusion from the source language. An English sentence such as *The property will be vacated...* requires restructuring (PEOPLE ALL MUST MOVE-OUT...) to clearly indicate the subject and object of the passive verb in ASL.

5. Structuring of Space, Pausing, Transition Markers and Cohesion: When properly done, aspects such as structuring of space, pausing, transition markers, and cohesion will aid immensely in the comprehensibility of the sight translation. For example, it is useful to sign an entire thought before breaking to look back at the source text, to show how one segment of the document is related to the next, to carefully establish the location of parties being discussed in the document, etc.

6. Chunking: Sight translation is a process, which begins –as all interpreting does – with input. In order to produce a meaningful sight translation, we must read for meaning. An axiom in the computer world fits nicely here: GIGO, which means "Garbage In, Garbage Out." I cannot interpret that which I do not understand. This means I must put my initial effort into comprehension of the print source text. Two strategies that assist in reading comprehension for sight translation are chunking and parsing. Chunking is simply dividing a sentence or paragraph into the smallest semantic units. For example: Each segment/ of this form/ must be filled out/ completely/ using/ only capital letters/ and blue ink/ and must have your Initials/ before you move on/ to the next segment.

It is important to chunk the material and to read for meaning, and then render that meaning deliberately, with careful attention to whole thought processing and natural prosody.

Marking the page or on a transparency over the page to cue for chunks can maximize chunking effectiveness. Interpreters can mark the source text with slashes, write gloss equivalents in the target language on the source text, mark the document to note segments or specific terms, to indicate emphasis, or main points, to assist memory or to mark transitions and/or order, such as writing numbers for each point. If writing directly on the document is ill-advised or not allowed, the use of paper-clipped transparencies (as were used for overhead projection) might be helpful. A clipboard, book, notebook or something hard to write on can make this process more efficient.

7. Parsing: Parsing is the restructuring of source text sentences into the syntactic structure of the target language. For example, the English sentence *Each segment of this form must be filled out completely* might be signed in ASL as DOCUMENT ALL, YOU FILL-OUT PART PART PART EACH COMPLETE.

8. Time Management: Time Management is another important skill in sight translation. Interpreters must manage the time, yet insist on sufficient time to do an adequate and effective job. With a conscious and deliberate approach, the work can be maximally effective and comprehensible, helping to satisfy our responsibility to the accuracy and completeness of the sight translation. We have some flexibility and control, but we must be as efficient as possible as often others are waiting for the completion of the sight translation effort before moving on to the next phase of their time together. Perhaps the sight translation is the precursor to an appointment to sign a contract or agreement. The sight translation might be in the midst of a court trial. Our speed and efficiency will be appreciated, allowing the events to move forward as quickly as possible.

9. Space Management: Space management is important for arranging appropriate yet private visual access for the deaf client to see the interpreter as well as the document, book or other printed materials.

10. Eye Contact / Checks for Comprehension: Appropriate eye contact and checks for comprehension allow sight translation to be more

effective. Eye contact maintains a sense of connection with the client. It is also essential for back channel information to check for comprehension and to ensure that we move at the appropriate pace for the clients' needs.

5. Quality concerns regarding sight translation output

Quality concerns regarding the sight translation output include:

1. Target Language Production: To attain our goal of a meaningful sight translation, target language production must be natural. Appropriate eye contact, clarity of signing, appropriate emphasis, and other markers of fluency should be characteristics of target language production.

2. Prosody: In sight translation, prosody can be choppy and unnatural, perhaps because the interpreter is focused on reading. There are common prosody intrusions in cohesion markers, with problems such as pausing appropriate to the source rather than the target language, or where pausing, cohesion markers and other markers of prosody are tied to interpreter comprehension or processing. Effective prosody has appropriate pauses, cohesion and transitions, creating natural rhythm with appropriate eye contact, clear and consistent structuring of space and movement

3. Additional Concerns: Obstacles to effective sight translation include rushing or allowing oneself to be rushed, engaging in inappropriate conversation with the client, insertion of one's own feelings or responses to the material, and unconscious breaches of confidentiality due to poor placement of the parties and visual availability to outsiders of the sight translation.

6. Summary

Effective sight translation means being deliberate, conscious, focused on meaning in both the source and target languages, aware of our effect, consistent and attentive to our effect on consumers and the illocutionary power equivalence between the source and target texts.

And, finally: Becoming more adept at sight translation requires one key undertaking, and that is to practice. Research on expertise indicates 10,000 hours of doing a task are required before one becomes an expert. We will be well served to start logging those hours now. Sight translation is an area of work well-deserving of our attention and effort.

References

Duenas Gonzalez R., V. Vasquez and H. Mikkelson 1992. *Fundamentals of Court Interpretation: Theory, Policy, and Practice*, Carolina Academic Press, Durham, NC.

Nicodemus B. 2009. *Prosodic Markers and Utterance boundaries in American Sign Language Interpretation*. Gallaudet University Press.

Pöchhacker F. and M. Shlesinger (eds) 2002. *The Interpreting Studies Reader*, London/New York, Routledge.

Stansfield Ch.W. 2008. Sight Translation – LEP Partnership Second Language Testing, Inc. Rockville, MD

Wilbur R.B. 2000. Phonological and prosodic layering of nonmanuals in American Sign Language. In H. Lane and K. Emmorey (eds), *The signs of language revisited: Festschrift for Ursula Bellugi and Edward Klima*, Hillsdale, NJ: Lawrence Erlbaum, 213-241.

Working Papers Series – The National Council on Interpreting in Health Care - Sight Translation and Written Translation: Guidelines for Healthcare Interpreters - The National Council on Interpreting in Health Care - www.ncihc.org © April 2009

Deaf translator: a new profession. Context and limits
Julia Pelhate

1. The context

1.1. The emergence of the profession

Since the Milan's Congress in 1880, there were many schools for deaf children developed throughout France. However, the education imparted was not very suited to the children's needs. Education was commanded by pure oralists and in some occasions delivered with a visual representation of the spoken language, for example cued speech. The educational level achieved by the deaf children was often very low.

Like several other European countries, France has not had many schools in which education was taught in sign language. There were and are very few schools were teachers use French sign language and written French.

According to the French National Federation of the Deaf (FNSF), there are circa 800,000 Deaf sign language users in France, many of whom have very low literacy skills. People with low literacy skills are women and men for whom the use of writing is not immediate, spontaneous, nor easy, and they avoid this mean of expression and communication as much as possible. The incidence of low literacy skills amongst Deaf people in France is a phenomenal rate: about 80% of Deaf people are considered illiterate and almost 60% of them are unemployed.

For most, writing in French is like writing in a foreign language, a second language. Their primary language (even if not their native language) is the Sign Language (SL).

In reality, the disability of Deaf people is not the inability to hear. Their disability is socially constructed, it is the fact that they are unable to read, write or even speak the "same language" as the hearing society in which they live in. It is a communication disability and not sensorial as many think. Living in France, we are all exposed daily to the French language, in the news, on television, in newspapers, via websites, and even food packaging are full of written French. Being illiterate, Deaf people are left out of society and out of the essential information.

The profession of Sign Language interpreter began to emerge about 25 years ago. The SL interpreter is not only intended to be a tool of accessibility and communication for Deaf people, it is also a bridge between two cultures and a tool of integration. More recently, a new profession has appeared: the Deaf translator/interpreter. This professional is not only a SL interpreter but it is the one who can truly state that they can work into their primary language: Sign Language.

Students in SL Interpreting Courses learn that it is best for a translator/interpreter to produce a translation/interpretation in their native language. Therefore, who is best placed to translate a French written text into sign language?

In 2004, our cooperative company WebSourd, which included two professional SL interpreters, had begun to look into the possibility to train Deaf translators. WebSourd had just created a website entirely accessible to Deaf people, with a combination of videos and texts. Initially, we produced a variety of clips, some of which were made by SL interpreters and some by Deaf native sign language translators. We tested them with the target users and eventually we recognised that the best possible way to disseminate accurate information to the Deaf community was through using a Deaf translator. The reasons we identified were nuances, fineness, and the ease to give life to the text in sign language.

In 2005, a course of study for Deaf translators was established. 6 years later, we have now 5 professional Deaf translators who have graduated with a Master's level. With a still evolving society, and due to the advancements of technology, the profession of Deaf translator is slowly becoming more visible even though it is still not fully recognized. With the rise of SL translators and interpreters, Deaf French people are finally in a position almost equal with the other French citizens. These very important professions are emerging in response to the strong need due to the low literacy skills of the Deaf community.

1.2. The WebSourd company and accessibility

I was one of the first students to benefit from the bilingual school in Toulouse. With bilingual education, the languages of education are sign language and written French. Thanks to this approach, I grew up with two primary languages: French Sign Language (LSF) and written French.

By acquiring a complete understanding of LSF through bilingual education, I could easily learn how to read and write in French, unlike most of Deaf people who have not had this chance. So I decided to join the company to become a Deaf translator. As is often said, what makes a good translator is the excellent knowledge of the 'target' language. This was for me another way to fight the low level of literacy in the community.

The first aim of our company, WebSourd, is to reduce the impact of the barriers to accessibility to society for the Deaf community. In order to achieve this target, we needed, at first, to reduce the number of Deaf people with low literacy.

We, therefore, created a website of world news, all with sign language videos and texts in French. The aim of this website is to give the possibility to Deaf people to see the news in the two languages. This opportunity may give them equal access to information as their hearing counterpart and at the same time the possibility to read and improve their written French.

A WebSourd Deaf translator also works to translate various public documents such as information from public libraries, the website of the mayor, the website of the bus company, information about flights at the airport, newsletters, various companies' intranet messages, etc. – in order to make as much information accessible to Deaf people as possible.

The Deaf translator is a relatively new profession. What places us at the forefront of this profession is the fact that there are right now only 5 qualified Deaf translators in France, and they all are employed by one company, WebSourd. Therefore, the work we receive varies immensely, consisting of a multitude of different documents ranging from simple translations of the news for the website to a challenging translation of a theatre play.

For each translation, we always begin by analysing the form and the method of translation required in order to deliver the best quality translation. Quality is one of the most important principles of our profession.

However, how can we, Deaf translators, be sure that we deliver a good quality translation, given the fact that we receive no support? The general principles of translation taught at the university are often not suitable for a translation into French Sign Language.

2. Translation into sign language

2.1. Translation into sign language: Skills

SL translation requires not only perfect knowledge of SL and translation skills, but also knowledge of materials, the medium we use, and the constraints that accompany such a type of translation.

When it comes to materials and medium, translators of other languages need a pen and paper or a computer to preserve their translation in writing. They can go back and make adjustments, corrections, or any other type of modification. They can always add or remove a word or a whole page and edit all subsequent pages. SL interpreters/translators, on the other hand, can only "video-record" their translation live. For SL translators, the final product is a video, or more precisely a 'SL-video' (a professional SL interpreter has recently conducted a study about this denomination, see Gache 2005). They cannot change a word without having to re-record the whole video. They cannot remove a part of a video clip because if they do that, they should also change all the subsequent translation. In this case, preparation is therefore even more vital than in the case of written translations. SL interpreters/translators not only need support for their preparation (internet, books, dictionaries, etc.), but must also have excellent memory skills in order to prevent incorrect words in their translation.

In any translation, the final product must be clean, clearly written "black on white" if text. For a SL translation, as the end result is a video, it must also be clean and intelligible.

Therefore, Deaf translators should know not only how to translate but also how to:

- present themselves in front of a camera;
- dress appropriately in order to give maximum clarity in the message portrayed (e.g. dark clothing and single colour; the background should be in a contrasting colour, for example in grey, for those viewers with reduced sight such as Usher syndrome, etc.);
- position themselves in front of a camera;
- set the lighting;
- understand and use a camera;
- transfer a video clip;
- edit films, etc.

We also need to be prepared for all kinds of translation under unusual conditions, 'expect the unexpected'.

2.2. Start from scratch

Since the emergence of Deaf translators, about 6 years ago, the work continues to evolve. We have encountered more than one type of obstacle, whether linguistic or others (i.e., material, medium, etc.). As SL translation is a new profession, there is very little support, if any available. There are no ethics, no set rules. Everything has to be started from scratch.

We rely on the ethical principles and rules of any other SL interpreter. However, our work is in many ways different, though complementary.

So, how do we choose, in our translation work, the correct lexicon (signs), retain the general sense and correct syntax of sign language?

How can we avoid alienating the Parisian Deaf community when choosing Toulouse's regional signs?

How can we make sure that the translation of a text is understood by a wide audience, where by audience we mean the thousands of different kind of Deaf people, with different language level and capability, level of knowledge, intellectual level, understanding of general culture, so that everybody has equal access?

These and other questions are always at the back of our minds when working on a translation. When we receive a commission for a SL translation, such as the one that came from the Mayor of Lille, we have to think about the end users, the majority of whom are in this case from Lille. What do we do when sometimes the target audience does not understand some of the signs that we use in Toulouse?

Also, should we resort to creative signing to represent something that we are not aware while in Lille there is already an established sign?

Do we "just" translate the text, or should we adapt it to allow the Deaf reader to understand the meaning behind it?

This type of translation is a linguistic mediation rather than a true translation. It is a cultural adaptation containing references, explanations, and a simplified translation. Given that Deaf people often have a lack of knowledge due to the education they have received, does the translator have to assume the role of a linguistic mediator?

In one occasion, I had to translate purely administrative statements, for a website about taxes. Even in French, these texts are often even confusing for hearing people. How should I make them understandable for Deaf people, who often do not have access to the concepts contained in administrative documents, where the majority of Deaf people with low literacy skills pass such papers to their hearing families or friends to deal with? Do we translate accurately what the complicated text says, or do we have the right to manipulate the meaning, providing some additional description so that the final rendering is more easily accessible? Are we ignoring the ethical principle: "to remain neutral and loyal to the original text"?

Do we have the right to create a new sign because we often find ourselves lacking a specialised lexicon? Is it our duty to invent new lexical items in sign language because there is not a Sign Language Academy in charge of such task and responsible to verify and validate new signs?

2.3. Some of the limitations of a SL translation

We are often asked to translate videos with commentary. The aim is to embed the SL translation in vision. In principle, it is a work of translation like others but it requires a considerable effort in terms of timing and linguistic choices.

Interpreters generally know that interpreting a text tends to result on a different length product, sometimes even a longer translation. In the case of a video, we have a major constraint: it is necessary that the SL translation is simultaneous and within the timing of the commentary. It is, therefore, necessary to have these pieces translated by a person whose primary language is SL. A job that requires high skill level with placements and economy with the signed sentences, all this requires a perfect mastery of SL. Often we are forced to resort to translate by omission, where redundant expressions or even whole sentences are dropped.

As there are only 5 educated and trained Deaf translators with a degree in France, teamwork and exchanges opportunities are therefore limited. There is the need for discussion and reflection on our work that is left unsatisfied at the moment.

We often work with hearing SL interpreters but in order to make progress, develop our skills and refine the nuances in SL with relation to French, we need more qualified Deaf translators.

Recently, some Deaf people (in most cases, they are just actors or SL teachers) are called in to provide translations even though they are not trained in interpreting or translating, just because they are cheaper. This is a very problematic issue that leads to a poor level of service with very obvious errors in the translations produced.

It seems that the profession of Deaf translator is, right now, in the same situation as SL interpreting 20 years ago, where SL interpreters had to campaign against using hearing people who just knew SL and who claimed themselves as SL interpreters.

Lastly, our company is working on a systematic SL translation through the Avatar technology, which uses a three-dimensional (3D) animate character. To make this 3D Avatar understandable, we must not only change some of the logic behind SL but also some of its rules. Indeed, one of the issues is that the human eye is not yet accustomed to artificial movements. We also have to work not on camera but in a strange molding suit and small reflective dots applied all over our faces and hands (Motion Capture System) (see Chaminade, Hodgins and Kawato

2007; Sofge 2010).

This new systematic technology has a beneficial impact on the SL translation. As I mentioned above, one of the peculiarities of a SL translation is that the final product is a SL-video. Translation is a profession that demands the translator to be on the border of invisibility. The translator usually should remain invisible to the reader. The more they remain invisible, the better is the end result. However, for translations into SL the final product is a video. The presence of the translator in vision has, therefore, the opposite effect of what all translators desire. The original text is often completely obscure to the viewers. We only see the translator and the final translation. Some users of our services even come to think that we are the authors of the original texts.

However, this modern technology can allow the Deaf translator to remain anonymous, to remain invisible. This technology is not perfect yet; we will hopefully be able to succeed in the near future.

3. Education at university level

The Centre for Interpreting and Translation (CETIM) of the University of Toulouse 2 – Le Mirail is now almost in the tenth year of existence in its present form, having been developed, and greatly expanded, from a postgraduate technical translation course.

The Centre welcomes students and future interpreters and translators in English, Spanish, Italian, and French Sign Language.

The University course now includes 5 years of studies, from Licence 1 to Master 2. The first three years are designed to give students solid basic skills in translation, interpreting, and linguistic mediation. The last two years are mostly focused on practices about interpretation and translation.

CETIM also welcomes deaf students wishing to become Deaf translators. The CETIM course is the same as for hearing interpreters – so that at the very end, the Deaf translator has the same skills and qualities as a hearing interpreter.

The courses are run in a mixed environment; deaf and hearing students attend lectures together. This allows them to exchange their knowledge and experience of their own respective languages.

In order to become a Deaf translator, it is necessary to undergo five years of study. The course comprises of:

- The basis of translation
- The methods of translation
- General and specific culture (such as political rights, international law, English political history, labour law, etc.)
- The use and work with video cameras
- Basic Computer skills
- The development of French Sign Language
- The development of French
- The methodology of the translation from French to LSF

The course with this programme started in 2011, and there are now four deaf students attending. Some of them will end after 3 years, License 3 - to become a language mediator, others will continue to Master 2.

In the future, we would like to open a course or a module to train Deaf interpreters: a perspective for the purpose of enriching the development of Deaf interpreters who can interpret between two different sign languages. These will hopefully have equal status as current hearing interpreters.

In conclusion, the SL translation profession is still like a young Deaf baby. There are still many things to discover, learn, and change. New experiences will come and with it, new challenges will arrive.

References

Chaminade T., J. Hodgins and M. Kawato 2007. Anthropomorphism influences perception of computer-animated characters' actions, *Social Cognitive and Affective Neuroscience* 2:3, 206-216.

Gache P. 2005. Traduction français ecrit langue des signes-video, Master 2 Thesis, Université Lille 3.

Sofge E. 2010. The Truth About Robotic's Uncanny Valley - Human-Like

Robots and the Uncanny Valley, *Popular Mechanics* (Posted on January 20, 2010; retrieved on March 20, 2011).

Requirements for translating films, in a multimedia context, from German into German sign language
Knut Weinmeister

1. Introduction

On passing the *Behindertengleichstellungsgesetz (BGG)* (German law against disability discrimination) which came into force on 1st May 2002, all public authorities were put under the obligation to design their Internet and Intranet services, homepages and other graphic programme surfaces, e.g. those of DVDs or menu screens, with barrier-free access (cf. *BGG* §11).

As a consequence of *BGG* §11, a regulation containing detailed information on how to implement barrier-free access was passed. This regulation, named *Barrierefreie Informationstechnik-Verordnung (BITV)*, came into force on 17th July 2002. It contains information about the groups of disabled people it refers to, the technical standards to be applied as well as deadlines for implementation and a potential technological assessment. It was only when the *BITV 2.0* was passed in September 2011 that the interests of Deaf people were taken into account and were thus given a legal basis. For instance, §3 of the regulation states that the internet or intranet homepage of a public authority must provide information in German Sign Language (*Deutsche Gebärdensprache*, DGS) about the content, navigation on the website, and any other of their website pages should be providing content in DGS. Furthermore, the regulation sets standards on the provision of information in DGS on the Internet or the Intranet, e.g. regarding the colour of the background as well as the clothing of the presenter, and the logo to be used for DGS.

Besides this legal recognition as per *BGG* 2002, the empowerment and increasing awareness of Deaf people regarding the status of DGS as an independent language has led to a wider acceptance of the language by society, particularly with respect to education, work, and public authorities. This resulted in a growing market for interpretation and translation services into DGS. Translations, which are fixed, take the form of sign language films.

This new legal situation and the wider acceptance by the society have resulted in the development of a market for translation service provision of sign language films in particular.

In this article, I will first list the main areas in which textual translations (including sight translations) are used. Then, I will outline the requirements that a translator has to fulfil, and adapt or modify to render them as applicable for sign language translations. In addition, I will discuss the question as to why, in this field, it is recommended to use Deaf translators.

2. What kind of texts are translated into sign language?

Due to legal regulations such as *BGG* 2002 and *Kommunikationshilfenverordnung* (regulation specifying the right to communication support, e.g. sign language interpreters) and as a consequence of the professionalisation of sign language interpreting, interpreting between spoken German and DGS is no longer the only option for transferring information between these two languages. In fact, translation between written German and DGS has been developing as an additional area in this respect.

Texts that are commonly translated into sign language come from three main areas. The first area is concerned with texts published by public authorities under the *BGG* (e.g. texts for the Internet, DVDs, or the Intranet), already mentioned in the introduction. The second one deals with texts which are used on-site, e.g. at the police stations, in court, or at a doctor's surgery. In such situations, sight translation is used, e.g. in the case of transferring an arrest warrant.

There is another area where translations can be produced but where no legal obligations exist. In this case, the provision of a translation in sign language depends on the goodwill of institutions or individuals who are concerned, for instance, with bilingual education and the inclusion of Deaf people into mainstream cultural and society. Their initiative and the budget available are significant factors in this respect. Texts for translation cover a miscellaneous of fields, ranging from children' books, leaflets to texts used for audio guides in museums. This generally includes everything that is printed.

3. Requirements for a translator working from German into DGS

In order to provide a correct[4] translation and to increase the usability of this translation by the Deaf community, translators have to possess a set of specific competences. In this chapter, I will outline what competences and skills are needed and what requirements a translator has to fulfil.

3.1 Requirements set by the EU commission

I have already mentioned some of the different translation perspectives and skills profiles of a translator and will now provide an extended picture by adding further aspects.

According to the EU, there are more than 285 translation programmes which all have different requirements, and the profession has been subject to ever greater changes. Therefore, the European Commission and its Directorate-General for Translation DGT have convened a commission of experts to develop a programme for a 'European Master's in Translation' (EMT).[5]

This EMT commission of experts has created a profile of competences that outlines general competences for all translators with different focal points. These 6 competences,[6] which will be explained in more detail later on, are the minimum requirements a translator needs to meet. They focus on multimedia communication and therefore they can also be applied to the translation of sign language films. The different focal points for translation are thus standardised and can be used as a basis to be built on in any language. Those who aim to work for a EU institution or in a similar field are confronted with a great amount of specialised texts (concerned with public authorities, economy, politics, etc.). These texts are similar to those published by the (German) federal authorities and therefore are relevant to this article as well as to the production of sign language films.

---

4 I will not go into detail here as to what constitutes a 'correct' translation.

5 http://ec.europa.eu/dgs/translation/programmes/emt/index_en.htm

6 http://ec.europa.eu/dgs/translation/programmes/emt/key_documents/emt_competences_translators_en.pdf

In total, the EMT commission of experts established 6 areas of competence which a translator has to possess as a minimum requirement. The diagram below shows the distinct areas of competence:

These areas are summed up below. In addition, I have included the specific requirements for translations from German to DGS that I have identified for each area:

1. Competences for a translation service provision

a. Interpersonal skills

- Being aware of the social role of the translator
- Knowing how to approach clients/potential clients (marketing)
- Knowing how to negotiate with the client (to define deadlines, fees/invoicing, working conditions, access to information, contract, rights, responsibilities, translation specifications, tender specifications, etc.)
- Knowing how to clarify the requirements, objectives and purposes of the client, recipients of the translation and other stakeholders
- Knowing how to plan and manage one's time, stress, workload, budget and on-going training (updating various competences)
- Knowing how to specify and calculate the services offered and their added value

- Knowing how to comply with instructions, deadlines, commitments, interpersonal competences, and team organisation
- Knowing how to work under pressure and with other experts, with a project leader (capabilities for making contacts, for cooperation and collaboration), including in a multilingual situation
- Knowing how to work in a team, including a virtual team

b. Production's skills

- Knowing how to create and offer a translation appropriate to the client's request, i.e. to the aim/skopos and to the translation situation
- Knowing how to define stages and strategies for the translation of a document
- Knowing how to define and evaluate translation problems and find appropriate solutions
- Knowing how to justify one's translation choices and decisions
- Mastering the appropriate meta-language (to talk about one's work, strategies and decisions)
- Knowing how to proofread and revise a translation (mastering techniques and strategies for proofreading and revision)
- Knowing how to establish and monitor quality standards

Requirements for translations from German to DGS concerning the area of translation service provision:

This area concerns the administration and negotiation competence between principal and agent as well as the ability to work in a team, which may include hearing translators, e.g. for the purpose of checking translations. Capacity for teamwork relates to freelance work as well as to employment.

2. Language competences

- Understanding grammatical, lexical and idiomatic structures as well as the graphic and typographic conventions of language A and one's other working languages (B, C)
- Knowing how to use these same structures and conventions in A and B languages
- Increasing sensitivity to changes in languages (useful for exercising creativity)

Requirements for translations from German to DGS concerning the area of language competence:

An excellent reading competence in the source language is required, as detailed in the section dealing with the textual dimension. An above average competence in the target language DGS is also necessary, especially with respect to the use of different registers as well as sociolinguistic factors.

3. Intercultural competences

a. Sociolinguistic skills

- Knowing how to recognise function and meaning in language variations (social, geographical, historical, stylistic)
- Knowing how to identify the rules of interaction relating to a specific community, including non-verbal elements (useful knowledge of negotiation)
- Knowing how to produce a register appropriate to a given situation, for a particular document (written/videoed) or speech (spoken/signed)

b. Textual skills

- Understanding and analysing the macrostructure of a document and its overall coherence (including where it consists of visual and sound elements)
- Knowing how to grasp the presuppositions, the implicit, allusions, stereotypes and intertextual nature of a document
- Knowing how to describe and evaluate one's problems with comprehension and define strategies to solve them
- Knowing how to extract and summarise the essential information in a document (ability to summarise)
- Knowing how to recognise and identify elements, values and references inherent in the cultures represented
- Knowing how to bring together and compare cultural elements and methods of composition
- Knowing how to compose a document in accordance with the conventions of the genre and rhetorical standards
- Knowing how to draft, rephrase, restructure, condense, and post-edit rapidly and well (in languages A and B)

Requirements for translations from German to DGS concerning the area of intercultural competence:

Competence in both languages and cultures is needed, relating to the sociolinguistic aspects and textual competence. Knowledge taken from the hearing culture is transferred to the Deaf culture.

4. Information collating competences

- Knowing how to identify one's information and documentation requirements
- Developing strategies for documentation and terminological research (including approaching experts)
- Knowing how to extract and process relevant information for a given task (documentation, terminological, phraseological information)
- Developing criteria for evaluation of vis-à-vis documents accessible on the Internet or any other medium, i.e. knowing how to evaluate the reliability of documentation sources (critical mind)
- Knowing how to use tools and search engines effectively (e.g. terminology software, electronic corpora, electronic dictionaries)
- Mastering the archiving of one's own documents

Requirements for translations from German to DGS concerning the area of information gathering:

Independent research for information found for example in books or software, and analysis of the source texts are also relevant when dealing with DGS. In addition to researching unknown signs from lexicons or special journals, it is necessary to be able to paraphrase texts in order to render them in DGS.

5. Thematic competences

- Knowing how to search for appropriate information to gain a better grasp of the thematic aspects of a document (cf. Information searching competence)
- Learning to develop one's knowledge in specialist fields and applications (mastering systems of concepts, methods of reasoning, presentation, controlled language, terminology, etc.) (Learning to learn)

- Developing a spirit of curiosity, analysis and summary

Requirements for translations from German to DGS concerning the area of thematic competences:

These concern the application of one's own expert knowledge to the source text, and with the willingness to attend further training in specialised areas.

6. Technological competences (mastery of tools)

- Knowing how to use effectively and rapidly and to integrate a range of software to assist in correction, translation, terminology, layout, and documentation research (for example text processing, spell and grammar check, the Internet, translation memory, terminology database, voice recognition software, etc.)
- Knowing how to create and manage a database and files

Requirements for translations from German to DGS concerning the area of technological competences (mastery of tools):

Since competences in this area have been listed with written language as a target language in mind, they are not directly transferable to translations into DGS. However, I have identified two further competences required for translation in a multimedia context, which are outlined in the following section.

3.2 Additional competences required for translating in a multimedia context

The following two competences have not been mentioned in section 3.1 above as they are directly related to the provision of translations into DGS in the multimedia field.

<u>Media technical competence</u>

Using cameras and technical editing such as cutting and embedding films into a homepage are important competences for a sign language presenter. This way, they will know e.g. when to pause, at what point the subtitles are shown, where specific contents on the DVD or the internet can be found and therefore what the technical elements are composed of.

Media presentation competence

Signing clearly and intelligibly, avoiding errors or 'stuttering' and signing freely are a must for the smooth production of sign language films.

4. Deaf translators

The Deutscher Gehörlosenbund (DGB) (German Deaf Association) recommends in its guidelines to use Deaf rather than hearing translators.[7] Not only the DGB, but also Signing Books[8] have outlined requirements in this respect. Due to acquiring sign language in a natural way at a very young age, Deaf people generally have a better aptitude than most hearing people for signing in front of a camera.

The use of Deaf translators has received little attention so far and is not mentioned explicitly in the guidelines either. Therefore, I would like to expand on the subject further in this section. All in all, there are 5 reasons that suggest that Deaf translators are most suitable for the job.

1. Given the choice between a Deaf and a hearing signer, Deaf people as the target group tend to prefer Deaf signers, irrespective of the translation aspect. There are two reasons for this, which are illustrated in the following quote from Signing Books (ibid.):

For the user tests in the UK, 14 adult Deaf viewers watched video-clips of two professional signers (one hearing, one Deaf) signing a short script.

Most subjects preferred the Deaf signer; they felt that the signer was fluent and natural and that they could understand her without too much concentration. The concepts were presented very visually, and she was clear in her BSL concepts and used a lot of facial expression.

The subjects thought that the hearing signer could do the job, but

---

7 Leitfaden für den Einsatz von DGS-Filmen: http://www.wob11.de/leitfaden-dgs-filme.html

8 http://www.signingbooks.org/doku.php?id=signers

they felt that 'something was missing'. One subject said she preferred the Deaf signer because she could identify with her as another Deaf person.

Deaf people can follow Deaf signers more easily and take in information better than from hearing signers. In addition, both are aware of their role and identity. Therefore, a Deaf signer can adapt more easily to the needs of the target group.

2. Language is evolving and changing constantly. Only native speakers have the mindset needed to translate a source text into the respective target language. Deaf translators have an above average language competence in DGS as the target language as they grow up using this language. CODAs, children of deaf adults, as well as near-native signers who learn sign language later on also have a comparable competence in DGS. However, most hearing translators have acquired DGS as a foreign language and have not grown up using it on a daily basis, which is why they have not had the opportunity to develop native language skills in DGS to a full extent.

In addition, translation theory generally recommends the target language to be the native language.[9]

3. Deaf translators possess sociolinguistic knowledge and a good awareness of registers concerning, for instance, the differences between the language used by the elderly and the young and the differences between the formal and informal use of language. They are familiar with DGS across all areas of life. In contrast, hearing translators may focus on a specific area in their work, e.g. education.

4. Jana Greschniok (2009: 80) also confirms: *„Die Vertrautheit mit der Zielkultur (insofern die Übersetzung in die Gebärdensprache erfolgt) ist eine der Stärken gehörloser Übersetzer."* (Familiarity with the target culture (insofar as the translation is produced into sign language) is one of the Deaf translators' major .) [my translation]. This describes the

---

[9] See Translation: getting it right – A guide to buying translations (english version), p.16; Übersetzung: keine Glückssache – Eine Einkaufshilfe für Übersetzungsdienstleistungen (German version), p.16; to be downloaded on the ITI's website: www.iti.org.uk/pages/advice/advice.asp

aspect of intercultural competence.

5. Stone (2007: 18) described differences between Deaf and hearing interpreters and translators regarding the translation process.

The process itself, the Deaf T/Is render the SL into signed BSL straight away and then re-render the information in signed BSL many times until it makes sense.

The hearing T/Is explain the process in English, thinking and reformulating in English before rendering the information in BSL one time only. The TL is not rehearsed.

The Deaf T/Is transferred the English source text directly into BSL, while the hearing T/Is first processed the English text before rendering it into BSL. Thus, Deaf people focus on processing the target language, while hearing people produce the target language based on their processing of the source language.

5. Summary

Deaf people have an above average competence in the target language and target culture, which is important for the sign language film as a final product and for the target audience. The target group favours Deaf signers even if they have not received specific training and have not learned translation strategies. In order to combine the target group and translation theory with each other, the Deaf translator has to increase their knowledge in the field of translation theory.

Obviously, not all Deaf people possess a language competence of this level or the other competences outlined in sections 3.1 and 3.2.

However, we should rather use the strengths of the native and near-native signers and expand them with respect to the seven competences mentioned above. For this purpose, it is useful to complete further training by attending the study course *Taube Gebärdensprachdolmetscher* (Deaf sign language interpreters) at the University of Hamburg in order to enrich the target group with new qualities of translation.

Furthermore, this is a possibility to open up new professional areas for Deaf people. Being native signers, they are given the responsibility for mainstream texts in their language, which also helps to raise awareness of sign language in society.

References

Greschniok J. 2009. Auf dem Weg vom Dienst an der Gemeinschaft zur Professionalisierung, unpublished thesis, University of Hamburg.

Stone Ch.A. 2007. Deaf Translators/Interpreters rendering processes - the translation of oral languages, *The Sign Language Translator and Interpreter* 1.1, Manchester: St. Jerome Publishing.

Barrierefreie Informationstechnik-Verordnung (BITV)
http://www.wob11.de/bitv.html, accessed on May 2, 2010

Behindertengleichstellungsgesetz (BGG)
http://www.gesetze-im-internet.de/bgg/BJNR146800002.html, accessed on May 2, 2010

Leitfaden für den Einsatz von Gebärdensprach-Filmen (2006), accessed on May 1, 2010, http://www.wob11.de/leitfaden-dgs-filme.html

Kommunikationshilfenverordnung
http://www.gesetze-im-internet.de/khv/BJNR265000002.html, accessed on May 2, 2010

Translation: getting it right – A guide to buying translations (English version); Über-setzung: keine Glückssache – Eine Einkaufshilfe für Übersetzungsdienstleistungen (German version), http://www.iti.org.uk/pages/advice/advice.asp, accessed on July 30, 2012

http://ec.europa.eu/dgs/translation/programmes/emt/index_de.htm, accessed on May 1, 2010

http://ec.europa.eu/dgs/translation/programmes/emt/key_documents/emt_competences_translators_de.pdf, accessed on May 1, 2010

http://www.signingbooks.org/doku.php?id=signers, accessed on May 2, 2010

Abstracts

This section contains the abstracts of the other contributors

How should a sign language interpreter prepare to perform a sight interpretation of a signed text?

Giuseppe Amorini

The issue that I have covered in my presentation is "Strategies for the translation of written texts in LIS." I'd love to share my personal experience with the participants.

To date I have used two types of strategies that relate to two different situations in which texts can be found: translation of books and subtitled television programs, in front of an audience of Deaf people with low literary skills.

Usually, I find myself translating texts that had been read and internalized, and where the interpretation into sign language is done in the register accessible to the audience.

The other situations I have found myself interpreting in are at the ENS (Deaf club) and with my Deaf family, interpreting films from the subtitles. This is because my family cannot access the subtitles in the way they are presented and because of their speed, so it is often my role to provide such access.

The two situations that I have presented are quite different. In the translation of written texts, the need to reflect the possible emotions and subjective expressions of the characters comes into play. In the translation of television programmes, the movements and expressions of the actors are already on screen, therefore all that is left for me to do is to provide access to the subtitles to support what is being watched.

So the techniques used in the two cases are different: in the case of subtitled programmes, translation is influenced by the images; in the case of written texts, the translation has more space for creativity but it is also more subjective.

Sight translation and sign language translation: two young and eager cousins of sign language interpreting?

Stuart Anderson and Donna Ruane-Cauchi

As a Sign Language Interpreting training provider, a module on sight translation has always been part of our interpreter development courses, covering a specific (non-compulsory) unit of the Signature qualification for sign language interpreting.

However, recently, Signature have moved to providing interpreting qualifications for Deaf interpreters and are currently looking into developing a qualification for sign language translation, which will be open to Deaf and hearing people with a high level of BSL and English. We have been part of this process and we shared in this presentation our thoughts on why we think a full qualification for sign language translation is timely and needed and how we think this qualification could work.

We looked at what we have been covering in our teaching of the one-day sight translation module for our interpreting courses and explored how course content has developed over the time we have been teaching this qualification.

The presentation then discussed reasons for expanding teaching on translation and extending from sight translation into other areas such as sight interpreting (via palantype and auto-cue for example) and other translation techniques, including building-up glossaries, preparation and review/evaluation methods and specific issues relating to translation between English and BSL. We also explored the need for expanding the specifications of the qualifications to cover the wider demands of sight translation and discuss reasons for making this module mandatory.

The presentation ended with an outlook to the way this new qualification may change the interpreting profession and how the range of skills in sign language professionals is being broadened. We believe that this is beneficial to the whole community of sign language professionals. We also explored new areas this may cover and new job opportunities which will arise in the future.

Interpreting scripted speeches: an examination of expert interpreters

Daniel Gile, Brenda Nicodemus, Laurie Swabey and Marty Taylor

Increasingly, signed language interpreters are called upon to interpret formal, public speeches, which are highly scripted and delivered as performances. Speeches, which are fully constructed prior to delivery, have linguistic characteristics that are different from spontaneous communication.

However, interpreters are rarely taught how to prepare or interpret speeches that are scripted. Furthermore, little research has been done to examine how expert interpreters handle the cognitive overload that may occur when rendering a scripted speech.

In our presentation, we explored these issues by sharing the results of a collaborative study conducted by researchers, who are also interpreters and interpreter educators, from France, Canada, and the United States (US).

The study examined how ASL/English interpreters prepared for and rendered a tightly constructed speech for a highly public event - the inaugural address of President Barack Obama. After interpreting the speech into ASL, each participant viewed their videotaped interpretation and engaged in a retrospective Think Aloud Protocol (TAP) about the work.

The presenters discuss the rhetorical devices used in this type of speech and the categories of preparation strategies identified through the analysis of the interviews with the ASL-English interpreters. Both theoretical and practical implications of the results are discussed and possible strategies are provided for educators and interpreter practitioners to prepare and render formal, scripted speeches.

Sign language translation as cooperative action: a theoretical model and an example from practice

Nadja Grbic, Karin Hofstätter and Christian Stalzer

In signed (as well as spoken) language interpreting, working in teams has been a standard practice for many decades. Due to highly complex cognitive demands and complex communicative situations, team interpreting is not only practised in many settings, it has also been a subject of research and an important component of interpreter training all over the world. This is one of the reasons we now know quite a lot about the processes of collaboration, diverse approaches to teamwork, and about various problems that might occur, as well as possible solutions.

With regard to sign language translation practice, the "younger cousin" of sign language interpreting, we do not know much about the processes involved. We know of the growing demand for translations of websites, tests, literature, to name but a few common examples, but there is only a handful of empirical studies, which tell us more about how those translations from a written text into a fixed sign language video are carried out.

This paper aims at filling one of these gaps by presenting the Theory of Translational Action by Justa Holz-Mänttäri, adapting and applying it to sign language translation and checking it against an example of a website translation from German into Austrian Sign Language. Holz-Mänttäri places special emphasis on the aspects of the action of the translation process, analysing the roles of participants and the conditions in which translations take place. One of her prime concerns is the question of expertise and cooperation. Based on Holz-Mänttäri's theory and the further development of her approach by Hanna Risku, we analysed the translation of a website into Austrian Sign Language which was done as a collaborative translation by a team comprising hearing and Deaf translators. In our analysis, we discussed both the individuals' roles and the situational conditions of the process, as well as some special characteristics of the finished product. As for the discussion of the product, we introduced Utz Maas' model of "Oral" and "Written" forms of discourse. What is essential for Maas is not writing as material action but writing as social action, which is to say writing carried out with a reader in mind who in turn will have to make sense of the written text. The difference between the "Written" and the "Oral" categories is therefore not based on material but on social distinctions and therefore seems to be valuable, also, for analysing translations into signed languages.

References

Holz-Mänttäri J. 1984. *Translatorisches Handeln. Theorie und Methode*. Helsinki: Suomalainen Tiedeakatemia.

Leneham M. 2005. The sign language interpreter as translator: challenging traditional definitions of translation and interpreting, *Deaf Worlds* 21:1, 79-102.

Maas U. 2010. Literat und orat. Grundbegriffe der Analyse geschriebener und gesprochener Sprache, *Grazer Linguistische Studien* 73, 21-150.

Metzger M. and B. Bahan 2001. Discourse analysis, in C. Lucas (ed), *The Sociolinguistics of Sign Languages*. Cambridge: Cambridge University Press, 112-144.

Napier J. 2006. Effectively teaching discourse to sign language interpreting students, *Language, Culture and the Curriculum* 19:3, 251-265.

Risku H. and R. Freihoff 2000. Kooperative Textgestaltung im translatorischen Handlungsrahmen, in A. Chesterman, N. Gallardo San Salvador, Y. Gambier (eds), *Translation in Context: Selected Contributions from the EST Congress, Granada 1998*. Amsterdam/Philadelphia: John Benjamins, 49-59.

About the contributors

Giuseppe Amorini

the second child of Deaf parents from southern Italy, received his MA degree in Philosophy in 2006 at the University Federico II in Naples and his Doctoral degree in Linguistics in 2012 at the University of Klagenfurt (Austria). He has studied for 9 months at the Gallaudet University (Washington DC), thanks to a Fulbright grant. He has taught, as an expert of Italian sign language (LIS), at the University of Salerno and the Istituto Universitario Orientale in Naples. He teaches on the course for school interpreters at the Università Suor Orsola Benincasa in Naples. He is the President of the Naples branch of ENS (Association of Italian Deaf people).

Stuart Anderson

is Director of Signamic, a specialist interpreter training centre, offering Signature qualifications in BSL Levels 1, 2, 3 and 6, as well as Interpreting and Translation at Level 6. He is a qualified BSL teacher, A1 assessor and also holds the V1 and V2 qualifications for internal and external verifying. Stuart is also a qualified and registered Sign Language Translator and holds full ASLI membership. He has been teaching sign language interpreters for many years and has extensive knowledge and experience as a sign language translator. He has contributed papers to several conferences on sign language interpreting and is contributed significantly towards the development of a new qualification and training programme for sign language translation, which is available to both Deaf and hearing people in the UK.

Carmela Bertone

graduated in *Literature and arts studies* at the University of Salerno in 1990. In 2007, she received her PHD in *Linguistics and Philology* with a thesis on noun phrases in Italian Sign Language. She teaches theory of Italian Sign Language (LIS) at Ca' Foscari University of Venice. As a specialized teacher for special needs, she teaches Italian language to deaf students in a middle school in Padua. She has worked on the grammatical description of LIS and on the syntactic analysis of noun phrases in LIS. She also works on the acquisition of Italian language by deaf children and adolescents and on the issues associated with translating of Italian into LIS and LIS into Italian.

Sarah Bown

is Senior Lecturer and Course Leader for the **B.A. (Hons.) Interpreting British Sign Language/English** programme at the University of Wolverhampton. Her current research areas include Sight Translation, Student Employability, Reflective Practice and Global Citizenship, and interpreter training pedagogy. Alongside her teaching portfolio, she works extensively across the UK in the area of interpreting and generic student work placement. She has three decades of experience within the field of deafness spanning private, public and charitable sectors which includes lecturing, training, consultancy and management of interpreting services. Her work as a qualified interpreter covered all key domain areas. A Fellow of the Higher Education Academy, Mentor for the **Institute of Learning Enhancement's** teachers in training and a member of efsli's newly formed Committee of Experts. She was awarded 'TEACHER OF THE YEAR' for excellence in learning and teaching pedagogy by the University and is the founder and facilitator of 'IRIS', International Research Interpreting Seminars Languages, based at the University of Wolverhampton.

Valeria Buonomo

is an Interpreter and a teacher of LIS interpreters (since 1995) on university and non-university Master's Courses. She obtained a degree in Educational Sciences in 2005 at Naples Suor Orsola Benincasa University, with a thesis on the Theory of Emotions, entitled: "The emotional dimension in the process of interpreting Italian sign language". In 2006, she worked as a planner and coordinator for the Master's Course for school interpreters at Suor Orsola Benincasa University, where from 2003 until 2006 she collaborated to teach "Special Education". In 2011, she obtained a doctorate from Naples Oriental University, with a thesis on the Theory of Languages and Language, entitled: "Language of the LIS, starting with interpreting problems". She has been collaborating since 2006 with the Sign Language Semiotics Department of Naples Oriental University and has been teaching since 2009 on the LIS course organised by the CILA at that university. She is a member of the Central Executive Committee of the ANIOS (Association of LIS Interpreters) and a member of the Entry Examination of this association. In 2010, she published *L'interprete di lingua dei Segni Italiana*, Hoepli Ed., Milan, with Pietro Celo.

Anna Cardinaletti

teaches Theoretical and Applied Linguistics, Italian Linguistics, and Clinical linguistics at Ca' Foscari University of Venice. She got her MA degree in Foreign languages and literatures in 1984 at the University of Venice and her Doctoral degree in Linguistics in 1990 at the University of Padua. She is the coordinator of the MA program in Language Sciences, and responsible for the curriculum "Linguistics for deafness and language disorders" in the same program. She is the director of the Master's Course in "Theory and techniques of translation and interpretation to and from Italian and Italian sign language (LIS)". She has published extensively on the comparative syntax of Romance and Germanic languages, and on the description and grammatical analysis of Italian and Italian dialects. She also works on the grammar of Italian Sign Language, the acquisition of Italian as a L1, the syntactic properties of translations into Italian, and on some syntactic properties of the Italian competence of deaf and aphasic subjects. She is the coordinator of research projects on the grammar of sign languages and on linguistic issues related to deafness.

Pietro Celo

a child of deaf parents, obtained a degree in Modern Languages in 1993 at Milan State University, with a thesis on experimental Pedagogy, entitled: "Practical aspects of interrogative sentences in Italian Sign Language". In 1999, he was a lecturer on the three-year course for support teachers at the Pontifical Catholic University of Ecuador in Esmeraldas. Since 2002, he has been a contract professor of Sign Language and the History and Culture of the Deaf at the Department of Language Sciences of Ca' Foscari University in Venice and since 2005 at Milan Bicocca University. He has been a consultant of the "Italian-Sign Language" Bilingual Project of the Teaching Department of Cossato (Biella) since 1994, where he is responsible of the coordination of the group of interpreters. He teaches Italian literature at the "Ranzoni" State Secondary School in Verbania, and heis a planner and teacher on courses for sign language interpreters some of which are organised by the Professional University School of Italian Switzerland (SUPSI) and the OPPI Association in Milan. In 2001, he authored for the Editore Kappa publisher of Rome "*Il maestro dei segni*", a charming parody on education of the deaf in the 19th century and, in 2009, for the publisher Cafoscarina of Venice "*I segni del '900*", a collection of Italian poems translated into sign language by the students on the advanced interpreting course at Venice University. In 2010, he wrote "*L'interprete di Lingua dei Segni Italiana*", Hoepli Ed., Milan, with Valeria Buonomo. From 2004-07, he was President for one term of office of the Italian Association of LIS Interpreters (ANIOS); he is currently a member of the Examination Board of the association.

Kristiaan Dekesel

has been a lecturer in Deaf Studies and Interpreting: (BSL/English) at the University of Wolverhampton since the early 90s. He is Head of the Department of World and Sign Languages and since 2010 became the Manager of Special projects for the division of business, community and International solutions. He lectures in Deaf Studies, Interpreting (BSL/Eng), War Studies, and Sign/General Linguistics. His current research interests are Think Aloud Protocols, verb classification, and battle field command during the Marlburian/Napoleonic wars. He is also a management committee member of the Centre for Translational and Transcultural Research.

Daniel Gile

former mathematician, has two PhDs, one in Japanese and the other in Linguistics. He has held a Professorship in various Universities in France and he is now a Professor at ESIT Université Paris 3 – Sorbonne Nouvelle in Paris. He is a scientific and technical translator and conference interpreter, and member of AIIC. He has sat on various editorial boards for a number of specialised journals, and he is now the editor of the CIRIN Bulletin. As a consultant, he has contributed to numerous advisory boards for academic purposes. Doctor Gile has published about 210 papers and written 3 books, as well as contributed to a number of collective volumes.

Nadja Grbic

studied linguistics and Slavic languages and is Assistant Professor at the Department for Translation Studies at the University of Graz, Austria. She teaches translation and interpreting studies and is currently preparing her post-doctoral dissertation (Habilitation) on the construction of sign language interpreters as an occupational group in Austria. Research topics include signed language interpreting, social issues of translation and interpreting, translation history, feminist translation, and scientometrics. She has conducted several research projects on signed language interpreting and sign language lexicography and developed a five-year full time training program for sign language interpreters at university level, which started in the autumn of 2002 at the University of Graz.

Karin Hofstätter

studied linguistics and Austrian Sign Language (ÖGS). She teaches Austrian Sign Language, Deaf Culture and sociology and translation as well as interpreting at the Department for Translation Studies at the University of Graz, Austria. With her deaf colleague Christian Stalzer, she has developed teaching materials for all levels of sign language instruction. For the last 15 years, she has been working on several research projects on signed language interpreting and sign language lexicography. She also works as a freelance sign language interpreter.

Sharon Neumann Solow

works as an interpreter, interpreter coordinator, performer, lecturer, author and consultant. Her career has taken her around the United States, and to Canada, Mexico, South America, Europe, Scandinavia, New Zealand and Australia. The author of two books – *Sign Language Interpreting: A Basic Resource Book* and *Say It With Sign* –Sharon also has written a number of professional articles and handbooks. Her television appearances include talk shows, variety shows and documentaries. She co-stars with her husband, Larry Solow, on the Emmy award-nominated NBC Knowledge series, *Say It With Sign*, which still airs throughout the United States. As the female lead in *The Electric Sign Company*, she and Gary Sanderson delighted audiences for over three decades. Sharon is a working interpreter, mostly in legal, community and conference settings, with a long history of classroom interpreting and educational interpreter training and administration. In court work, she specializes in work with deaf people with limited English and ASL proficiency. Her travels and some of her conference work have involved the use of international gesture interpreting (a gestural, pantomimic form of communication across language barriers). She also has been involved in the education of spoken language interpreters and interpreter educators through the Monterey Institute of International Studies. An active member of the RID (Registry of Interpreters of the Deaf) and CIT (Conference of Interpreter Trainers), Sharon holds the Specialist Certificate: Legal, as well as NAD's SIGN (Sign Language Instructor) Comprehensive Permanent Certificate. Sharon is the 1987 recipient of the national Virginia Hughes Award for outstanding contributions to the field of sign language interpreting, the 2005 President's Choice Award from NAOBI (National Alliance of Black Interpreters), the 2005 President's Award from the Registry of Interpreters for the DEAF, and the 2010 Mary Stotler Award from the Registry of Interpreters for the Deaf and the Conference of Interpreter Trainers.

Brenda Nicodemus

is currently Assistant Professor in the Department of Interpretation at Gallaudet University and the Director of the Interpretation and Translation Research Center. She has worked professionally as an interpreter since 1989 and holds a PhD in Educational Linguistics from the University of New Mexico. Brenda has taught interpreting at various postsecondary institutions and has presented both nationally and internationally. Her publications include *Prosodic Markers and Utterance Boundaries in American Sign Language Interpreting* (Gallaudet University Press, 2009) and, with co-editor Laurie Swabey, *Advances in Interpreting Research* (Benjamins, 2011).

Julia Pelhate

born deaf, she was educated in a bilingual school (Written French and French Sign Language), hence her strong base of both languages. After studying Art History, and travelled to the discovery of Asian cultures, she came back to further her studies. Her focus was Translation and Interpreting at the University of Toulouse. Believing that her knowledge and skills should be made available to translate information for the benefit of Deaf people that find it difficult to access the written language, she joined the cooperative society WebSourd in 2006. She has graduated with a Master of Translation and Interpretation (2008) and is now the translators team leader of the company.

Donna Ruane-Cauchi

is a British Sign Language/English Interpreter, MRSLI, MASLI, interpreting trainer and interpreting A1 Assessor. Over the past ten years, she has worked as a sign language interpreter, interpreting trainer, mentor and assessor in a wide range of UK settings. She is the Chair of ASLI's CPD team and delivers training to trainee and qualified interpreters specifically in the domains of Sight translation and Theatrical Interpreting.

Christian Stalzer

who is Deaf, is Lecturer at the Department for Translation Studies at the University of Graz, Austria. He teaches Austrian Sign Language (ÖGS), Deaf Culture and Deaf Sociology, and translation skills. His research interests include sign language grammar and sign language teaching. Together with Karin Hofstätter, he has developed teaching materials for Austrian Sign Language. He has been working on several research projects on signed language interpreting and sign language lexicography and is currently preparing his MA thesis on negation in ÖGS.

Laurie A. Swabey

has a PhD in Linguistics from the University of Minnesota and has been a certified interpreter since 1976. Currently, she is Professor of ASL and Interpreting and Director of the CATIE Centre at the St. Catherine University, Minnesota (USA). As an invited lecturer and presenter, Dr. Swabey has shared her expertise and research on interpreting education and healthcare interpreting nationally and internationally. Her recent publications include *Educating Healthcare Interpreters* (Gallaudet University Press, 2012) with co-editor Karen Malcolm and, with co-editor Brenda Nicodemus, *Advances in Interpreting Research* (Benjamins, 2011). She has been the recipient of a number of awards, including the RID Research Award in 2010 (with B. Nicodemus) and the St. Catherine University Carol Easley Denny Award in 2011.

Marty M. Taylor

has a PhD in Educational Psychology from the University of Alberta (Canada). Her former educational background was also on the same subject. Marty has been a Certified Interpreter since 1977 and has achieved certification with both RID (USA) and AVLIC (Canada). She is the President and Chief Executive Officer of 'Interpreting Consolidated' – Edmonton, Alberta (Canada). She has been, also, chair and instructor in many ASL/English interpreting programmes in colleges in the USA and Canada. She is an interpreters' coordinator at local, national and international programmes and events. She has collaborated and offered her services as a consultant to a number of cooperation between Canada and USA. Dr Taylor is also a well-known author and presenter with special interests in educational interpreting and video relay interpreting and related topics. She has been the recipient of a number of awards including the AVLIC – Edward C. Bealer of Merit Award for outstanding contribution.

Knut Weinmeister

graduated in 2002 in teaching at special needs schools (deaf education and education for pupils with a learning disability). From 2004 to 2009, he was a research assistant and doctoral student for sign language education at Humboldt Universität in Berlin. In 2003, he began working at the company GEBÄRDENWERK, where he is CEO, managing partner, producer and translator of various sign language films, online and offline. From 2011 until present, he has been the CEO of the company SIGN FACTOR. In September 2011, he passed the *Staatliche Prüfung* (state exam) for sign language interpreters carried out by the *Amt für Lehrerbildung* (office for teacher training) in Darmstadt after attending the further education programme *Taube Gebärdensprachdolmetscherinnen und -dolmetscher* (Deaf Sign Language Interpreters) at the *Institut für Deutsche Gebärdensprache und Kommunikation Gehörloser* (Institute for German Sign Language and Communication of the Deaf), University of Hamburg.

www.ingramcontent.com/pod-product-compliance
Lightning Source LLC
Chambersburg PA
CBHW071513150426
43191CB00009B/1518

"In this book, David Schreiner interweaves personal travel adventures, biblical interpretation, and thoughts on larger issues pertaining to ecology, creation, and Scripture. From his visit to the Galapagos Islands to his study of the Genesis creation accounts, this book inspires readers to reflect upon the nuances of the biblical text and carefully consider the role of humanity in creation."

—**Julianne Burnett**, Assistant Professor of Old Testament, Asbury University

"Schreiner offers Christian readers a unique entry to the subjects of creation care and natural history by taking them along his family vacations to the Galapagos Islands—a multi-island nature preserve and famed site of Darwin's early observations. We get to hear Schreiner's thoughts with him as a theologian walks among lounging seals, frolicking penguins, and lumbering tortoises, pondering the complex and sometimes competing calls to care for God's human and natural creation. There is no stinging rebuke for ravaging the planet, but rather a call to be drawn in to the beauty of God's creation, recognize the legitimacy and complexity of competing needs, and seek ways to honor our calling as caretakers of the garden. *Frigate Birds, Sea Lions, and Darwin* is a fun, introspective, insightful, and easy read."

—**Gregg Davidson**, Professor of Geology and Geological Engineering, University of Mississippi

"David Schreiner diverts from his normal academic contributions to produce an intriguing contribution to scholarship. Far more than a travel log, this book attempts to reconcile ecology, evolution, and creation theology to create an engaging interaction with the difficult topic of human origins."

—**Samuel C. Long**, Professor of Old Testament, Great Lakes Christian College

"This book discusses exegesis, theology, science, faith, culture, and politics. But it is not a theological treatise, cultural apologetic, political manifesto, or deconstruction story. It is a memoir that brings the reader along on a personal faith journey where family vacations and conversations prompt maturing, nuancing, rethinking, and freshly exploring a truly Christian response to controversial issues like evolution and ecology. A helpful reflection—and makes me want to visit the Galapagos Islands!"

—**KENNETH J. TURNER**, Professor of Old Testament and Biblical Languages, Toccoa Falls College